対訳

銀行員のための

『論語と算盤』
とSDGs

渋澤 健 著
Ken Shibusawa

一般社団法人 金融財政事情研究会

◆対訳について

　キーワードは逐語訳とし、全体を通しては直訳調を避け、意味を通した訳としています。

◆論語と算盤 の表記について

　和文は、本のタイトルを指す場合は『　　』に入れ、コンセプトを表す場合は、英文カッコの"　　"に入れています。

　英文は、本のタイトルを指す場合はイタリック体（斜体）太字にして"　　"に入れ、コンセプトを表す場合は大文字にして"　　"なしにしています。

目　次

Table of Contents

渋沢栄一の
"論語と算盤"の
現代的意義は SDGs

PREFACE ● RONGO and SOROBAN
is SDGs

SDGsバッジを付けていますか？

　街を歩いていると時々、スーツの襟に大きな丸い、カラフルなバッジを付けている人を見かけることがありませんか。

　それは「SDGsバッジ」です。「SDGsにしっかり取り組んでいます」ということを社外にアピールするのに、多くの会社が使っています。

　あるいは、皆さんのなかにも、付けていらっしゃる方は多いのではないでしょうか。

　あれだけカラフルなバッジですから、知らない人からしたら「いったい何なのだろう」となるでしょう。そういう人から質問を受けたら、「これは国連で定められた、SDGsという人類共通の目標です。2030年までに誰一人取り残さない世の中を皆がともにつくるために達成するべき目標を、色別にしたものです」とお答えください。

　そのような場面で皆さんに、気をつけていただきたいことがあります。「いや〜、会社にいわれたから付けてます」と決していわないように。SDGsバッジを付けるうえで大事なことは、「自分コト」として腹に落ちていることです。誰かにいわれているからではありません。

　一人ひとりが自分コトとしてこの取組みに興味をもち、知らない人に伝えることによって、SDGsはどんどん世界的規模で広まっていくのです。

　SDGsバッジの円周にはたくさんの色が付けられていますが、あの色の数だけ目標があるのです。

Are You Wearing the SDGs Badge?

The "SDGs badge" is that round, colorful pin badge, worn on the lapel of a suit jacket of business persons. It is a common sight in almost any city in Japan. Many companies use the badge to appeal to the public "Our business is aligned with the SDGs."

As the badge is so eye-catching, people may ask "What is it?"

The proper way to answer this question is, "It is a symbol for the SDGs, common goals of humanity adopted by the United Nations. It represents color-coded set of goals that declares No One Left Behind by 2030 in the world."

Please do not simply say "It is my company's policy to wear it."

It is essential that everyone feels ownership to achieve the SDGs. The SDGs can only be achieved on a global scale, when each one of us feels this ownership. If you think it is important, you will share your excitement with others.

If it still sounds a little vague, let's think about it relative to Japan and the world.

Japan is a society with a declining population, while the world population will continue to follow an increasing trend. By 2020, the global population will be 7.8 billion, which is projected to be 8.5 billion by 2030, and 9.7 billion by 2050.

その数、実に17です。

SDGsとは「Sustainable Development Goals」の略で、これを日本語にすると、「持続可能な開発目標」になります。これだけでは漠然としていて「ちょっと意味がわからない」という人も少なくないと思います。

これから日本は人口減少社会に入っていきますが、それとは逆に世界人口はどんどん増加傾向をたどっていきます。2020年の世界人口は78億人ですが、これが2030年には85億人に、2050年には97億人になると予測されています。このように世界人口が急増するなか、これまで70年以上にわたって続けてきた先進国型の経済成長モデル、つまり大量生産・大量消費型の経済を今後も行えば、環境問題や食糧問題、資源問題が深刻化するのは目に見えています。まさに地球の危機です。

だからこそ、「持続可能な開発目標」が必要になるのです。ここでいう「持続可能」とは、地球における人間の生活のことを指しています。私たちにとってかけがえのない地球が、子々孫々の代まで誰にとっても住みやすく、美しい惑星であり続けるための目標です。

SDGsは世界各国の満場一致で、2015年9月の国連総会において正式に採択され、17のゴールと169のターゲット、232の指標が設けられました。すでに6年前のことです。その達成年限は2030年であり、刻々と迫っています。

17のゴールは、次の一覧表のとおりです。

【図表　17のゴール】

目標1 〈貧困〉	あらゆる場所のあらゆる形態の貧困を終わらせる。

With the world's population soaring, it is clear that environment, food and resource are problems that will become more serious if we continue with the economic growth model, which has been in place for more than 70 years.

That is why we need the Sustainable Development Goals. The term "sustainable" here refers to the lives of ourselves on Planet Earth.

The SDGs with 17 goals, 169 targets and 232 indicators were formally adopted unanimously by the nations in September 2015 at the UN General Assembly. That was nearly 6 years ago. The year to achieve SDGs, 2030 is approaching rapidly.

The 17 goals are listed below.

【Chart 17 Goals】

1 No Poverty	End poverty in all its forms everywhere
2 Zero Hunger	End hunger, achieve food security and improved nutrition, and promote sustainable agriculture
3 Good Health and Well-being	Ensure healthy lives and promote well-being for all at all ages
4 Quality Education	Ensure inclusive and equitable quality education and promote lifelong learning opportunities for all
5 Gender Equality	Achieve gender equality and empower all women and girls
6 Clean Water and Sanitation	Ensure availability and sustainable management of water and sanitation for all

目標 2 〈飢餓〉	飢餓を終わらせ、食料安全保障及び栄養改善を実現し、持続可能な農業を促進する。
目標 3 〈保健〉	あらゆる年齢のすべての人々の健康的な生活を確保し、福祉を促進する。
目標 4 〈教育〉	すべての人に包摂的かつ公正な質の高い教育を確保し、生涯学習の機会を促進する。
目標 5〈ジェンダー〉	ジェンダー平等を達成し、すべての女性及び女児の能力強化を行う。
目標 6 〈水・衛生〉	すべての人々の水と衛生の利用可能性と持続可能な管理を確保する。
目標 7〈エネルギー〉	すべての人々の、安価かつ信頼できる持続可能な近代的エネルギーへのアクセスを確保する。
目標 8 〈経済成長と雇用〉	包摂的かつ持続可能な経済成長及びすべての人々の完全かつ生産的な雇用と働きがいのある人間らしい雇用（ディーセント・ワーク）を促進する。
目標 9 〈インフラ、産業化、イノベーション〉	強靱（レジリエント）なインフラ構築、包摂的かつ持続可能な産業化の促進及びイノベーションの推進を図る。
目標10〈不平等〉	各国内及び各国間の不平等を是正する。
目標11〈持続可能な都市〉	包摂的で安全かつ強靱（レジリエント）で持続可能な都市及び人間居住を実現する。
目標12〈持続可能な生産と消費〉	持続可能な生産消費形態を確保する。
目標13〈気候変動〉	気候変動及びその影響を軽減するための緊急対策を講じる。
目標14〈海洋資源〉	持続可能な開発のために海洋・海洋資源を保全し、持続可能な形で利用する。
目標15〈陸上資源〉	陸域生態系の保護、回復、持続可能な利用の推進、持続可能な森林の管理、砂漠化への対処ならびに土地の劣化の阻止・回復及び生物多様性の損失を阻止する。

7 Affordable and Clean Energy	Ensure access to affordable, reliable, sustainable and modern energy for all
8 Decent Work and Economic Growth	Promote sustained, inclusive and sustainable economic growth, full and productive employment and decent work for all
9 Industry, Innovation and Infrastructure	Build resilient infrastructure, promote inclusive and sustainable industrialization, and foster innovation
10 Reduced Inequality	Reduce income inequality within and among countries
11 Sustainable Cities and Communities	Make cities and human settlements inclusive, safe, resilient, and sustainable
12 Responsible Consumption and Production	Ensure sustainable consumption and production patterns
13 Climate Action	Take urgent action to combat climate change and its impacts by regulating emissions and promoting developments in renewable energy
14 Life Below Water	Conserve and sustainably use the oceans, seas and marine resources for sustainable development
15 Life on Land	Protect, restore and promote sustainable use of terrestrial ecosystems, sustainably manage forests, combat desertification, and halt and reverse land degradation and halt biodiversity loss
16 Peace and Justice Strong Institutions	Promote peaceful and inclusive societies for sustainable development, provide access to justice for all and build effective, accountable and inclusive institutions at all levels

| 目標16〈平和〉 | 持続可能な開発のための平和で包摂的な社会を促進し、すべての人々に司法へのアクセスを提供し、あらゆるレベルにおいて効果的で説明責任のある包摂的な制度を構築する。 |
| 目標17〈実施手段〉 | 持続可能な開発のための実施手段を強化し、グローバル・パートナーシップを活性化する。 |

（注）　外務省資料より

　国連では、この17のゴールを5つのPに分類しています。

　People（ゴール1〜6）……基本的な人間のニーズ

　Prosperity（ゴール7〜12）……豊かで充実した生活

　Planet（ゴール13〜15）……責任ある自然保全

　Peace（ゴール16）……人権が保持される平和

　Partnership（ゴール17）……さまざまなセクターのグローバルなパートナーシップ

　一方、日本政府が2016年に設けた「SDGs推進本部」は、SDGsの目標を日本人の思考にあわせるために、次の5つの原則にも集約しています。

①　**普遍性**……国内実施と国際協力の両面で率先して取り組む。

②　**包摂性**……誰一人取り残さない。

③　**参画性**……全員参加型で取り組む。

④　**統合性**……統合的解決の視点をもって取り組む。

⑤　**透明性**……定期的に評価、公表し、説明責任を果たす。

　本書を執筆しているのが2021年7月ですから、残された時間はあと9年ほどです。「どこか遠い国のことだね〜」などと思っていては、実現できるものもできなくなります。また「自分が抱えている仕事と何が関係あるの」では近視眼的な状態に陥り、時代の大きな

17 Partnerships to achieve the Goal	Strengthen the means of implementation and revitalize the Global Partnership for Sustainable Development

https://sdgs.un.org/goals

The United Nations also classified these 17 goals into 5 P's.

People: (Goal 1 -6) Basic Human Needs

Prosperity: (Goal 7-12) Well-Being for Fulfilling Life

Planet: (Goal 13-15) Responsible Nature Conservation

Peace: (Goal 16) Preserving Human Rights and Dignity

Partnerships: (Goal 17) Global Partnerships Across Sectors

In addition, the "SDGs Promotion Headquarters" established by the Japanese government in 2016, the 17 goals were grouped into 5 principles, probably with the intention to align the SDGs with the mindset of the Japanese people.

Universality: Take the lead domestically and internationally to implement.

Inclusive Approach: No one left behind.

Participatory Approach: All stakeholders play a role.

Integrated Approach: Fostering interactions and synergies among various issues.

Transparency and Accountability: Disclose assessments on the progress made regularly.

If you think SDGs is "about someone else in some distant

流れを見落としてしまうかもしれません。

　現在、日本は新しい時代への節目に立っています。その新しい時代における銀行の役割とは何か。その新しい時代で変わらなければならないこと、そして変わらないものは何か。その新しい時代の銀行、そして銀行員のあり方を見極めるという視点を、このSDGsの5つの原則に沿って皆さんとともに考えることが、本書の趣旨であります。

SDGsに通じる渋沢栄一の教え

　2021年2月からNHKで、「青天を衝け」という大河ドラマがスタートしました。主人公は、渋沢栄一です。ちなみに私は、栄一の玄孫（やしゃご）に当たります。「孫の孫」のことです。

　銀行に勤めていらっしゃる皆さんなら、渋沢栄一の名前ぐらいは耳にしたことがあるでしょう。日本に初めて民間銀行をつくったのが、渋沢栄一です。いまのみずほホールディングスの前身である第一国立銀行を33歳の時、明治6（1873）年に設立し、そのトップに就任しました。以後、栄一はおよそ500の民間企業と600の社会的事業の設立にかかわりました。そのため、「日本資本主義の父」などといわれています。

　さて、渋沢栄一が提唱していたのは "論語と算盤" です。栄一の名前を、現代においても有名にしているのは、それがタイトルと

country," then we cannot achieve what can be achieved. If you think "What does this have to do with my work," you will miss the huge changing of the tide in our lifetime.

Presently, Japan is standing at a very critical point in time for the new coming era.

What is the role of banks in that new era?

Some things must change in that new era, but some other things will stand the test of time. Let us think together, using these SDGs 5 principles as a guide, about the purpose of the bank and those working there in this new era.

Eiichi Shibusawa's Legacy and the SDGs

From February 2021, a popular NHK Sunday night drama series is featuring "Seiten wo Tsuke" (Reach for the Blue Sky) . The main character is Eiichi Shibusawa, my great great grandfather.

If you are working at a Japanese bank, you have probably heard his name before. He established the first private bank in Japan, "The First National Bank of Japan" (predecessor to Mizuho Bank) in 1873, 6th year of the Meiji Era. He was 33 years old.

In his lifetime Eiichi has been involved in the establishment of about 500 private companies and 600 social enterprises, and therefore, is said to be the "Father of Japanese

なった本の存在が大きいと思います。ちなみにこの本は栄一本人が一言一句を書き連ねたものではなく、栄一の講演集であり、大正5（1916）年に初版が出版されています。いまから100年ぐらい前に、栄一が残した言葉です。

「冒頭、SDGsの話から入ったのに、なぜいきなり渋沢栄一の話に飛ぶのか」と思った方もいらっしゃるでしょう。

ちゃんとした理由があります。栄一が『論語と算盤』のなかで語った言葉の現代的な意義が、SDGsにほかならないからです。

『論語と算盤』を通じて栄一が唱えたのは、「道徳経済合一説」といわれるものです。この言葉の意味を知るためには、"論語"が何を意味しているのか、"算盤"が何を意味しているのかをあらためて理解する必要があります。

まず、"論語"。名前ぐらいは聞いたことがあると思います。中国春秋時代の思想家だった孔子と弟子の会話を記録したもので、孔子の名言集といってもよいでしょう。

「我、十有五にして学に志す。三十にして立つ。四十にして惑わず。五十にして天命を知る。六十にして耳順う。七十にして心の欲するところに従えども矩を超えず」

「故きを温めて新しきを知る」

「過ぎたるは及ばざるがごとし」

このあたりが有名な言葉です。恐らく日本人のほとんどが、これらの言葉を一度はどこかで学んでいると思います。「故きを温めて新しきを知る」は、「温故知新」という四字成語で知られています。ここからもわかるように、『論語』の中身は、人としての物事の考え方や道徳について述べたものです。ちなみに『論語』の伝世最古の写本は日本にあるそうで、そういう意味では日本人が初めて手に

Capitalism.

Eiichi Shibusawa advocated *"Rongo* (The Analects of Confucius) *and Soroban* (The Abacus)", and published a compilation of his public speeches with this title in 1916 (5th year of the Taisho Era). As such many people identify Eiichi with *"Rongo and Soroban"**

(*Note: Throughout this book I will refer to "The Analects of Confucius" as RONGO because it is a mouthful, and "The Abacus" as SOROBAN)

So why take a leap from the modern day SDGs to Eiichi Shibusawa of the past? The reason is simply, that the modern day interpretation of Eiichi's words that he left in *"Rongo and Sorban"* and other writings are in synchronicity with the SDGs. They are essentially saying the same thing, in a different language, in a different era of Japan.

RONGO and SOROBAN is the "integration of morality and business."

First, a quick description of RONGO. It is called the "Analects" because it is a record of conversations between Confucius, an ancient Chinese philosopher from the Chunqiu Era (approximately 771 to 403 BC) and his disciples.

Most Japanese have studied famous quotes from *"Rongo"* in their school days. It is a way of thinking and acting ethically for humanity.

On the other hand, SOROBAN refers to business. You need to count how much money you are making, and as a result, business is usually seen as cutthroat. If you want to

した書物かもしれません。

　一方、算盤は「ソロバン勘定」などという言葉があるように、商売のことを指しています。商売の世界は、まさに「生き馬の目を抜く」世界であり、ともすれば「金儲けのためなら手段を選ばず」ということになりがちです。

　『論語と算盤』は、商売人がこのようなダークサイドに陥らないようにするための警世の書といってもよいでしょう。栄一は『論語と算盤』を通じて、「道義を伴った利益を追求するべきだ」と提唱しました。

　道徳を意味する"論語"と、商売を意味する"算盤"。

　本来、これらは相反する要素を多分にもっています。その一見矛盾した状態において異分子を融合させて新しい創造を促すことが"論語と算盤"です。

　商売で儲けようと思ったら、「少々、道徳に反することでも致し方ない。見えてないからやってしまえ」などと考えてしまう場合があるかもしれません。

　実際問題、商売をするうえで道徳ばかりを重視していると、「儲かる案件も儲からなくなる」おそれがあります。つまり道徳心と商売は、水と油の関係であり、決して融合しないものと多くから思われ続けてきました。ただ、その想いを貫いて融合させたのが、渋沢栄一の91年の人生でした。

　持論ですが、渋沢栄一の思想の本質は一言で表すことができます。それは、「と」の力です。これに対するもう一つの大切な力もあります。それは、「か」の力です。

　「と」は and であり、「か」は or です。

　「か」は二者択一の場面で用いられます。「上か下」「右か左」「行

make money, you choose all means to attain it.

Eiichi Shibusawa wanted, through *"Rongo and Soroban,"* to prevent business merchants from falling to the dark side. His belief was that business merchants must also endear moral interests.

At first glance, RONGO and SOROBAN appear to have conflicting elements. When thinking about making money in business, cutting corners a bit on morality seems acceptable. In fact, there is usually concern that profitable businesses will not be as profitable if you emphasize morality. After all, we are in business, not philanthropic activities.

For many, morality and business seem like water and oil. It simply doesn't mix.

However, Eiichi Shibusawa's thinking is in a way, quite simple. The essence can be expressed with just one word, "AND."

Eiichi is showing us the importance of the power of "AND."

There is another very important power, and that is "OR."

"Up OR down", "right OR left", "go OR stop". The power of "OR" increases efficiency, so it is essential for managing an organization. It is also necessary for analysis. And, currently as I write this book, knowing whether you are "negative" OR "positive" with the corona virus is extremely important.

The "power of OR" divides into parts, so it makes it easier

くか止まるか」という具合になりますが、いずれも二者択一です。「か」の力は効率性を高めますので組織運営に不可欠です。物事を分析するときにも必要です。また、現在のコロナ禍において陰性「か」陽性「か」を把握することはきわめて重要です。

分断することによって「か」の力を発揮できます。分断するから複雑なものがわかりやすくなります。でも、分断すると、それ以上の化学反応を阻止していることになります。つまり、新しいクリエイション、創造がない。

これに対して「と」の力は融合です。いままで組合せができていなかった「AとBをあわせる」ことができれば、それまで存在していなかった新しいクリエイションになります。「AとBをあわせようとしても」何も起こらなかったところに、あるきっかけや条件が整うと、そこに化学反応が起こり、新しい創出があることを、皆さんも体験したことがあるでしょう。

渋沢栄一は「日本の資本主義の父」といわれますが、「資本主義」という言葉を使っていませんでした。栄一が唱えたのは「合本主義」でした。まさに「合わせる」「本」（もと）で、新しい社会（価値）を創造することでした。

"論語と算盤"の考え方もまったく同じです。道徳心と商売を融合させることによって、道徳心をもって商売をすることの大切さを、先の「道徳経済合一説」という言葉で、世の中に広めていったのです。

栄一は『論語と算盤』のなかで、このように指摘しています。

「正しい道理の富でなければ、その富は完全に永続することができぬ。ここにおいて論語と算盤という懸け離れたものを一致せしめることが、今日の緊要の務と自分は考えているのである」

to understand complexity.

Yet, because it divides, interaction stops and there is no more "chemical reaction." In other words, there is no new creation.

In contrast, the power of "AND" is combining. It may look like an unrealistic combination at the outset. Maybe nothing happens.

However, if a certain catalyst or certain conditions appear, a "chemical reaction" occurs and a new compound may form. That is a new creation.

As mentioned earlier, Eiichi Shibusawa is known to be the "Father of Japanese Capitalism." Yet, it is interesting to note that he didn't use the word "capitalism" (shihon-shugi).

He used the word, "gappon-shugi". In kanji (expression using Chinese characters), "gappon" is two characters "combine" and "foundation." In essence, "gappon-shugi" is the principle of integration, to create a new society of a modern Japan.

"Rongo and Soroban" is essentially saying the same thing. It is a principle of integrating morality AND business.

In his book, *"Rongo and Soroban"*, Eiichi observes the following.

"If wealth is not achieved through the proper way of doing things, then it will not endure the test of time. That is why it is important for us today to make efforts to integrate Rongo and Soroban, which appear to be so

この言葉は『論語と算盤』の冒頭にある「処世と信条」という章に出てくるのですが、私はこの言葉のなかの**「その富は完全に永続することができぬ」**が一つのキーワードだと考えています。

また、第7章の「算盤と権利」の章には、「合理的の経営」という教えがあり、次の言葉が書かれています。

「仮に一個人のみ大富豪になっても、社会の多数がために貧困に陥るような事業であったならばどんなものであろうか、如何にその人が富を積んでも、その幸福は継続されないではないか。故に国家多数の富を致す方法でなければいかぬというのである」

これは、まさにSDGsが唱える「誰一人取り残さない」ですね。SDGsが採択される100年ぐらい前から渋沢栄一は同じような考えを唱えていたのです。

栄一は決してお金儲けを否定していないということが大事です。むしろ、その意欲をもつことは重要だと考えています。ただ、商売人が稼ぎの手段を選ばず、儲けを独り占めしてしまい、大多数の人々を不幸に陥れてしまっては、結果的に商売人自身の幸せにもつながらないということをいっています。

「永続」と「継続」。つまり、栄一が『論語と算盤』のなかで最もいいたかったことをいまの時代の文脈で表現すれば、それは「持続可能性＝サステナビリティ」です。

まさに、SDGsの最初の「S」の部分です。そして渋沢栄一のライフワークとは、よりよい社会を築くこと、「D」（開発）であり、それが「G」（目標）でありました。

『論語と算盤』にはもう一つ、SDGsを語るうえでの重要なキーワードが含まれています。

それは「インクルージョン」です。**「仮に一個人のみ大富豪に**

far apart."

This word appears at the beginning of the first chapter, "Conduct and Principles" of *"Rongo and Soroban"*. The take away here is the key phrase, **"endure the test of time."**

Also, in Chapter 7, "Rongo and Rights" in a speech manuscript titled "Rational Management", Eiichi declares the following:

"If only one individual were to become wealthy, yet the rest in society suffers in poverty, what kind of business is that. Even if he is accumulating wealth, his well-being will not last. Therefore, we must find ways to bring wealth to many."

Eiichi said, "leave no one behind," just like the SDGs, but about 100 year before its adoption.

It is important to note that Eiichi never denies making money. Rather, he stressed that motivation factors are important. However, his warning is clear. If a merchant does not regard the means of his earnings, takes all the profits for himself, and the majority of people falls into misfortune, then this will not lead to his own well-being.

In other words, what Eiichi wanted to express through *"Rongo and Soroban"* in the context of the current era is, in fact, "sustainability".

The first "S" in SDGs is sustainability. The life work of Eiichi Shibusawa was to launch a new era for Japan, which is "D"(development). This was his "G" (goal).

なっても、社会の多数がために貧困に陥るような事業であったなら
ばどんなものであろうか」という上記の一文は、まさにこのインク
ルージョンを指しています。

　インクルージョンは、日本語では「包摂性」と訳されています
が、１％が生き残るために99％が犠牲になるような社会は、当然の
ことながらサステナブルではありません。サステナブルな社会を構
築していくためには、SDGsの目標の一つである「誰一人取り残さ
ない」という精神、つまりインクルージョンが大事であり、サステ
ナビリティとインクルージョンはセットになっていると考えられま
す。

　"論語と算盤"は、渋沢栄一のいまから100年以上も前の思想であ
りますが、SDGsが掲げているサステナビリティとインクルージョ
ンという２つの重要なキーワードを内包しているという点におい
て、"論語と算盤"の現代的な意義は、まさにSDGsそのものであ
るとさえいえると思います。

20世紀的成功モデルの限界

　ミルトン・フリードマンという経済学者をご存じでしょうか。金
融にかかわっている人なら一度は、その名前を耳にしていると思い
ますが、米国の有名な経済学者です。1976年にはノーベル経済学賞
を受賞しました。

　フリードマンさんは「マネタリスト」であり、政府の裁量的な財
政政策について反対の立場をとってきました。景気が悪くなると政
府が財政出動して需要を創造し、それによって景気は再び回復へと

Eiichi Shibusawa's lifework RONGO and SOROBAN is exactly what we call in our modern-day language, the SDGs.

It is also clear from his words above that Eiichi Shibusawa believed that "inclusion" was necessary to bring about a new era for Japan. A society where 1% attains the wealth and the 99% is left behind is just not sustainable.

Remember, Eiichi questioned "When wealth is accumulated, while the rest in society falls into misfortune, what kind of business is that." It is clear Eiichi believed inclusion was essential.

Eiichi believed that sustainability and inclusion was of utmost urgency for the well-being of a new society. That was his message 100 years ago through *"Rongo and Soroban"*. This message is still very relevant in our present world that is trying to achieve the SDGs.

Limitations of the 20th Century Success Model

Milton Friedman is renowned economist who was awarded the Nobel Prize in Economics in 1976. If you work in the financial market industry, you probably have heard of him.

Dr. Friedman was a "monetarist." He basically opposed direct government intervention such as fiscal policy. He did not agree with the theory or policy that encouraged the government to create demand, in order to stimulate growth and

向かうという考え方は間違っていて、あくまでも貨幣の供給量と利子率によって景気は循環するという考え方を貫いた人です。

徹底した市場原理至上主義者といってもよいでしょう。それは企業の社会的な存在意義についての考え方にも貫かれていて、それはたった一つ、「利益の最大化」であるというのが、フリードマンさんの考え方です。そして、この世の価値のあるものはすべてマネタイズでき、市場で合理的な価格で取引できるというのです。

私は、ノーベル経済学賞の受賞者に喧嘩を売るつもりは毛頭ありませんが、フリードマンさんのいうことには一理あると思う反面、企業の社会的な存在意義は、本当に利益の最大化だけなのだろうかという疑問もあります。

たしかに、企業のあり方を、利益最大化する社会インフラであるととらえると、事業のいろいろなことが財務諸表などで可視化できて分析上では便利です。

でも、その企業には大勢の「人間」が働いています。人間は感情の生き物ですから、フリードマンさんがいうように、効率的、合理的に利益を最大化するためだけに働く存在であるかと疑問を覚えるのです。

皆さんはどうですか。皆さんが働いている銀行は営利企業ですから、たしかにリスク・リターンを考慮しながら利益の最大化を目標にして全員が力をあわせて日々、働いていらっしゃるでしょう。しかし、利益を最大化させることだけが、皆さんが入行した動機ではなく、長年、お勤めしている理由でもないでしょう。

自分たちが関係している人たちの幸せを持続させていくために働いているところも、少なからずあるはずです。最も身近な関係者は家族であり、会社の同僚であり、会社の取引先、ひいては株主も含

spending. He persisted that the economic activity was based on the amount of money supplied and the rate of interest.

He was a hardcore proponent of the free markets. He believed that the only social responsibility of business, the purpose of existence was "maximization of profits." He believed anything of value could be monetized and traded freely in a market.

I have no intention of picking a fight with Nobel laureates. And, I think some of his thinking makes good sense. However, I do not agree with his thinking that the purpose of existence of a business in society is just about maximizing profits.

Certainly, it is useful for analysis to categorizing a company as an entity for "profit maximization" or "social infrastructure". However, there are many "people" working in a company. Because humans are creatures of emotion, I wonder if, as Mr. Friedman declared, people always work efficiently and rationally only for profit maximization.

Banks need profits to survive. And it is quite important for people that work there to think about the risk-return profile of their work activities in order to maximize profitability. However, did you join your bank just for the bank's profit maximization? Is that why you have been working there for so many years?

You must have some feeling that you work for the well-being of people with whom you have a relationship

めて、幅広いステークホルダーの幸せを実現し、それを維持してい
くために、日々の仕事に従事している自分もいるのではないでしょ
うか。

　もう少し、利益の最大化について考えてみましょう。

　利益の最大化が正義だった、もっと簡単な時代がありました。20
世紀はまさにそういうわかりやすい時代だったと思います。

　しかし、21世紀に入って20世紀的成功モデルの弊害が、いろいろ
なところで顕在化してきました。

　資源不足は、かつては石油をはじめとする化石燃料や鉱山資源な
どが、世界的な経済発展によって不足することを指していました
が、いまでは世界的な人口増加を受けて食糧不足にまで及ぶように
なってきました。

　経済発展は人々にたくさんの利便性を与えてくれましたが、同時
に地球環境は悪化の一途をたどっています。

　さらに、経済発展による恩恵を誰が享受しているのかを考えたと
き、そこには救いがたい格差の問題があることに気づきます。

　たしかに世界経済は成長していますし、これからも成長していく
とは思います。しかし、そこには大勢の取り残された人たちがいる
という事実から目を背けるわけにはいかないでしょう。

　まさに、20世紀的成功モデルが限界を迎えているのです。

　そして多くの人たちが、そのことに気づき始めました。

　2011年9月17日、米国のウォール街で「ウォールストリートを占
拠せよ」運動が行われました。これは2008年のリーマンショックの
煽りを受けて、若者は就職できずにいるのに、自分たちの欲望を満
たすためにリスキーな金融取引を行った投資銀行を救済するために
税金が投入されたことへの不満が爆発したものでした。

through the course of your work. Those may be stakeholders such as family members, company colleagues, business partners, and perhaps even shareholders.

In the 20st century there were not too many questions being raised about profit maximization of businesses. It was easy to understand.

However, in the 21st century, the 20th century successes have started to raise some concerns.

Shortage of fossil fuels, mining resources, food resources all because of successful global economic development to maximize profits. Economic development has given people a lot of convenience, but at the same time, global environment is being degraded.

Furthermore, when we think about enjoying the benefits of economic development, we realize that there is an unspeakable problem of inequality.

Indeed, the global economy is growing, and I think it will continue to grow, but we cannot ignore the fact that there are many people being left behind.

It looks as though the 20th century success model has reached its limits.

And many people have begun to notice.

In September 2011, "Occupy Wall Street" movement took place on Wall Street in the United States, fueled by the Lehman shock of 2008. When young people were unable to find jobs, discontent exploded over the tax cuts to bail out invest-

今回のコロナ禍においても、「ブラック・ライヴズ・マター」という、黒人に対する暴力や人種差別の撤廃を訴える運動が行われました。また白人至上主義者を中心とした群衆が米国議会を乗っ取るという前代未聞の暴動やアジア人に対するヘイト・クライムが相次いでいます。

　これらすべての根底に、経済発展の陰で取り残された人たちのフラストレーションが溜まり溜まって、何かのきっかけで爆発したといえるでしょう。

　このような時代の流れのなかで、いよいよもって20世紀的成功モデルの一つだった市場原理至上主義は、通用しなくなってきました。私たちは、新しい21世紀型の経済モデルを模索しなければならない状況に直面しているのです。

　皆さんは、宇沢弘文さんという経済学者をご存じですか。日本人でいちばんノーベル経済学賞に近いといわれていた方で、実はお若い時に前出のミルトン・フリードマンとシカゴ大学で同僚の関係でもありました。

　その宇沢先生の著書の代表作に『自動車の社会的費用』があります。いまも岩波新書で版を重ねていて、世間で関心が高まっています。新しい時代の到来によって、渋沢栄一の思想と同様に、宇沢理論がリバイバルしているのです。

　この本が出版されたのは1974年のことです。日本のモータリゼーションが花開いて日本人の生活が日々豊かになっていた時期に、宇沢先生は日本の経済成長を支えてきた自動車の普及によって生じる公害問題や交通事故など社会的費用を数値化し、経済学の問題として提起しました。

　多くの日本人が自動車という道具を手にして高い快適性と利便性

ment banks that made risky financial deals to satisfy their profit maximization desires.

In the current Covid-19 Crisis, "Black Lives Matter" demanded for the elimination of violence and racism against black people. Even white people rioted, and took over the U.S. Capital. Hate Crimes against Asians increased.

These are some of the cries and outbursts from those who felt they have been left behind in the shadow of economic development.

It appears the simple 20th century model for economic growth will not be able to answer to these cries. We have to seek a new 21st century economic model.

Dr. Friedman in his younger days had a Japanese colleague at the University of Chicago. His name was Hirofumi Uzawa. He was said to be the closest Japanese person to the Nobel Prize in Economics.

In 1974, He published "The Social Cost of Automobiles," which is still in print today. At the time the book was published, Japanese motorization was blossoming and Japanese people's lives were getting wealthier day by day. However, Dr. Uzawa questioned the economic growth, by quantifying social costs like pollution and automobile accidents.

Dr. Uzawa argues that while many Japanese enjoy comfort and convenience because of the automobile, there are actually social costs or "externalities" in economic theory, and that burden has been largely passed on to low-income people.

を享受する裏側に、実はさまざまな社会的費用という、経済理論では考慮しない「外部性」の存在のあることを明らかにしました。特に低所得者層にその社会的費用の負担が大きく転嫁されてきたというのが、宇沢先生の主張です。

つまり日本が高度経済成長期でどんどん豊かになるなかでも、実は取り残された人たちに対して社会的費用が転嫁され続けている不平等が生じていることを明らかにしたのです。いまから50年近く前に出版された本ではありますが、いま読み返してもまったく古さを感じさせないのは、時代がようやく宇沢先生の考え方に追いついてきたからではないでしょうか。

ステークホルダー資本主義の時代

2019年8月、米国大企業のCEOが200名ほど参加する「ビジネスラウンドテーブル（BRT）」が、新しい「企業の目的に関する声明」を発表し、その内容が話題になりました。

この組織は1972年に設立され、1978年から定期的に、「企業統治に関する原則」を発表しています。その基本原則は1997年からずっと、「企業は主に株主のためにある」というものでした。

ところが2019年8月に発表された声明は、これまでの「株主第一主義」から「ステークホルダー主義」に大きく舵を切ったものになりました。ここでいうステークホルダーとは、「顧客」「従業員」「取引先」「地域社会」「株主」のことを指しています。

そして2020年1月に開催されたダボス会議（世界経済フォーラム）では、「ステークホルダー資本主義」が主題に掲げられました。

In other words, even as Japan was becoming more and more affluent during the period of rapid economic growth, there were people being left behind. This book was published nearly 50 years ago, and it looks as though the times have finally caught up with Dr. Uzawa.

The Age of Stakeholder Capitalism

In August 2019, the "Business Round Table"(BRT), a business organization of about 200 CEOs from large U.S. companies, released their "Corporate Purpose Statement".

BRT was founded in 1972 and has regularly published its "Principles on Corporate Governance" since 1978. From 1997, BRT has declared that "companies exists primarily for shareholders".

However, the new statement was different. It shifted from "shareholder first" to "stakeholder capitalism". Stakeholders for business include "customers," "employees," "business partners," "local communities," and " shareholders."

At the Davos Conference (World Economic Forum) held

このステークホルダー資本主義について、いまから150年近く前から言及していたのが、渋沢栄一でした。

　前述したように彼は日本で初めて民間銀行を創設しました。1873年のことです。元号だと明治6年です。明治維新によって新しい日本ができてわずか5年後に、栄一は第一国立銀行を設立しました。

　当時はまだ「銀行」という言葉さえなかったので、いうなればいまのスタートアップ企業のようなものでした。栄一は、まだ世間からあまり認知されていなかった銀行という企業の役割を世の中に広めるため、次のようなたとえ話を用いました。

　「銀行は大きな河のようなものだ。銀行に集まって来ない金は、溝にたまっている水やポタポタ垂れている滴と変わらない。せっかく人を利し国を富ませる能力があっても、その効果は現れない」

　お金は世の中を良くする資源になりうるものだけれども、資源が離散している状態では大した力にはなりません。

　しかし、一人ひとりの少額のお金が銀行に集まれば、いずれお金の流れとなり、それが他のお金の流れとあわさることによって大河のような大きな流れになり、世の中を変える原動力をもつようになる、というのです。

　これが日本の資本主義の原点です。「資本主義」というと、1％の人たちを富ませるために99％の人々が犠牲になる、取り残されるという、非常に暗いイメージがつきまとうのですが、栄一が考えた資本主義はそうではありませんでした。

　1人の資産家だけではなく、多数から少額のお金を集め、それを今日よりも良い明日を実現させるために循環させていくというイメージを思い描いていたのだと思います。だから栄一は、資本主義という言葉を使わず、「合本主義」という言葉を用いました。

in January 2020, "stakeholder capitalism" was also the main theme for discussion.

As mentioned earlier, Eiichi Shibusawa created the first private bank in Japan. At that time, nobody knew what a "bank" looked like. Therefore, Eiichi described it to the public in this manner.

"A bank is like a big river. Money does not gather at the bank is no different from a puddle of water or dripping dew drop. Even though it has the ability to benefit people and enrich the country, that effect will not be realized."

Money can be a resource that makes a better society. However, if it does not flow like a big river, its potential for great impact will not materialize. A dew drop gathering at a bank that eventually becomes a big river can deliver that impact.

This is the origin of capitalism in Japan.

Usually, capitalism has a very dark image where 1% of people enjoying the benefits at the expense of the 99% that are being left behind.

But, the image that Eiichi had for the potential of capitalism was that even tiny dew drops can be empowered to enrich the wealth of the entire nation. This is the concept of "gappon-shugi" as mentioned earlier.

Although there is a limit to what each company or individual can do, if like dew drop, they gather for a common

また栄一は、その生涯を通じておよそ500の株式会社と600の社会事業を立ち上げたのですが、これもいうなれば「大河の一滴」と同じ発想です。

　一社一社、あるいは一人ひとりではできることが限られてしまうけれども、たくさんの会社、さまざまな人が集まれば、世の中を動かす原動力になると考えたのです。それも都市部だけでなく、日本全国隅々にまで成長性のある資金を循環させようというのが、栄一のもともとの発想でした。ここにも、取り残される人を出さないという点で、SDGsの考え方が垣間みられます。

　つまり資本主義は株主のためにだけあるのではなく、世の中のさまざまな人のためにあるということを、栄一は自分の生涯を通じて行ったさまざまな活動を通じて、世の中に伝え続けました。渋沢栄一が提唱した「合本主義」とはまさにステークホルダー資本主義につながるものであり、そこに『論語と算盤』とSDGsの連関性が認識できるのです。

SDGsは地域金融機関にとって生き残りのキーワード

　地域金融機関はいま、再編の渦に巻き込まれようとしています。国策として、地域金融機関の再編はこれから進められていかざるをえないでしょう。

　なぜ地域金融機関の再編が必要なのでしょうか。

　この点については、実際に現場で働いていらっしゃる皆さんのほうがよくご存じかと思います。**人口減少**です。

　地方の人口が減少傾向をたどれば、その地域の経済圏は縮小して

purpose then, big changes for a better society is forthcoming.

Here, too, you can glimpse the idea of the SDGs in Eiichi Shibusawa.

Eiichi believed and made efforts to convey to the world that capitalism exists not only for shareholders, but for the benefit of all. Therefore, Eiichi Shibusawa's "gappon-shugi" (gappon capitalism) is stakeholder capitalism of today, and *"Rongo and Soroban"* and the SDGs are singing the same tune.

SDGs and the Survival for Regional Financial Institutions ～～～

In the coming years, it is clear that regional financial institutions will be caught up in a storm of restructuring. Goverment policy have made it clear that this is one of the priorities.

The demographic shift in Japan where we will see an acceleration of **population decrease** is one of the main drivers of the need for this restructuring in the industry. Because

いきますし、それに伴ってその地域で活動していた企業の役割も縮小せざるをえません。こうした流れのなかで、地方企業のなかには廃業を余儀なくされているところもあります。

　しかし、金融機関の場合、そう簡単に廃業を選択するわけにはいきません。基本的に地域金融機関の大半は営利企業ではありますが、金融という社会インフラの一端を担っている以上、行政側からしても、そう簡単に廃業させるわけにはいかないのです。自然と、近隣県にある複数の地域金融機関同士で合併する動きが出てきました。

　ただ、再編も、単なる規模の経済を目指すものだとしたら、何の意味もありません。複数の地銀が合併して、たとえば預金や貸付の残高がメガバンクに並んだとしても、メガバンクに勝てるのかといわれれば、それはかなり厳しい面があると思います。

　このまま座して死を待つわけにはいきません。変わらなければならないことは、どの地域金融機関もわかっているのです。ただ、どのように変わればよいのかというところで、多くの地域金融機関は、悩んでいる最中であり、さまざまな取組みを模索しているのだと思われます。

　地域金融機関が変わっていくための答えが、実はSDGsの5つの原則に含まれているのではないでしょうか。普遍性、包摂性、参画性、統合性、そして透明性です。この原則を経営層だけでなく、現場で働いている地域金融機関の行員一人ひとりが自分コトとして理解し、行動することが大事です。

　ここ数年、「イケている」会社のなかに「パーパス」という言葉を用いるところが増えてきました。企業はビジョン、ミッションを掲げて、その実現に向けて日々の仕事に取り組んでいますが、ビ

population growth had been the main engine for domestic economic growth in Japan, the deterioration of the population in regional communities will obviously have negative impact on economic activity, and hence for regional financial institutions as well.

However, regional financial institutions just can not sit on their hands and wait for their deathbed. All of them realize that changes are necessary. Yet, they have not figured out how they can change.

I believe that some of the answer for the regional financial institutions can be found in the 5 Principles of the SDGs, universality, inclusive approach, participatory approach integrated approach, and transparency & accountability.

Over the past few years, "purpose" has been a buzzword in corporate management.

Companies have always used "vision" and "mission" in their corporate philosophy but more and more they are using "purpose."

"Mission" and "purpose" are often used interchangeably and sound like similar concepts regarding the existence of that company. Therefore, a little bit difficult to understand the difference.

There is a quite simple yet very clear difference between the two.

Mission is "What we do." The word "mission" is originated from a religious context. It was God's mission, and

ジョンやミッションに並んでパーパスを設ける企業が増えているのです。

ミッションとパーパスの違いは、ちょっと似ているのでわかりにくいのですが、ミッションは What we do、つまり「われわれは何をするべきなのか」ということです。ミッションという言葉はもともと宗教上の言葉なので、いうなれば神のお告げと同じで、それを忠実に執行することが大事です。軍隊でもミッションという言葉を使いますが、それはどのような難題が課されても絶対に達成しなければならない、という非常に強い強制力をもっています。

宗教上でも、軍隊上でもミッションにもう一つの共通点があります。ミッションに問うてはならないのです。「なぜ」がないのです。

これに対してパーパスは Why we do、つまり「われわれはなぜやるのか」という問いかけであり、それに対して自分の答えをきちんともっていることです。3年ぐらい前に米ハーバードビジネスレビュー誌の解説を読んで納得しました。つまり存在意義に対する問いかけといってもよいでしょう。

別な見方をすると、ミッションはどこか「やらされている感」があるのに対し、パーパスは自分コトとしてとらえないと成立しない面があります。地域金融機関に照らしていえば、「なぜこの地域にわれわれは金融機関として存在しているのか」という問いかけがパーパスであり、行員一人ひとりがその問いかけに対する答えをしっかりもっているかどうかによって、地域金融機関の存在価値が決まってきます。どのような逆境に直面したとしても。

ここから先の章で、日本政府が設けた SDGs の5つの原則である普遍性、包摂性、参画性、統合性、透明性に、渋沢栄一の思想の代表作である『論語と算盤』も融合させることで、特に地域と密着し

therefore faithful execution is important. It is also used in the military in the same way. It is important to execute despite the difficulties and challenges.

In this context, you never question the mission. There is no "Why."

About 3 years ago, I read a commentary in the Harvard Business Review magazine that beautifully describes the difference between "mission" and "purpose."

Purpose is "Why we do." It is having the question to check your company's and your existence in society and having a clear answer for it.

In other words, "mission" make you feel like someone else is ordering you to do it, whether you may not want. On the other hand, with "purpose", it is you that have the ownership of why you are doing it.

So, as the management or employees of a regional financial institution you have to ask yourself, "Why do we exist here?" If everybody can answer that question with his own words and will, then that institution's existence in the regional community is solid, despite all the challenges.

And in order to confirm the purpose for regional financial institutions and those working there, I believe the 5 principles of SDGs mentioned previousy offer a good framework to ask the question "why."

In the following chapters, we will take a journey together using the framework of the 5 principles of the SDGs: univer-

ている金融機関のこれからの時代のあり方の Why について、皆さんご自身の答えを見つけていただきたいと願っています。

したがって、ここでお断りしておきますが、本書は地域金融機関向けの SDGs 解説本やハウツー本でもありません。「どうやって」SDGs を達成するのかは、それぞれの銀行員の実践をふまえてご自身の頭で考えていただきたいからです。

「なぜ」が、会社にいわれたから、上司にいわれたからではなく、自分コトとして表現できていないのであれば、「どうやる」かは、自分自身、自分の銀行、自分の地域にとって本質的な意味があるといえないからです。

SDGs の 5 つの原則を用い、「なぜ」というパーパスの再確認を促すために大勢の地域金融機関の経営トップ等からインタビューにご協力をいただきました。それぞれの貴重なご発言は匿名で掲載してありますが、多くの気づきをいただきました。一言でいえば、それは、もっと良い機関になれる、もっと良い地域社会のためという熱い想いです。

1917（大正 6）年、『論語と算盤』が出版された翌年に、渋沢栄一は東北振興会会長として北陸・東北六県を18日間かけて巡回します。その際に、栄一は唱えました。

「国の繁栄には地方の振興が欠かせない」

「地方振興には現地の奮起努力が不可欠」

「銀行の発展は実業の隆盛があってこそ」

渋沢栄一の地域社会および地域金融機関への高い期待は明らかです。時代が変わっても、この期待は変わらない、いや、むしろ高まっていると思います。

どうぞお付き合いくださいませ。

sality, inclusive approach, participatory approach, integratory approach, transparency & accountability, in conjunction with Eiichi Shibusawa's *"Rongo and Soroban"*. Hopefully, along the way, you the reader can find your own answers to the "why".

Please take note, this is not an SDGs commentary book or a "how-to book" for regional financial institutions. How to achieve the SDGs should be done by you, since you are the one who is offering the day-to-day services in your community.

This "why" should not be because the company says it. It should not be because the boss says it. It should be your own expression. If you don't have your own expression for the "why", the "how to" really has little meaning for yourself, your bank, and your regional community.

I was fortunate to have the cooperation of many top management executives of regional financial institutions to gather my thoughts for this book. Their valuable opinions are introduced anonymously in the text, but I certainly learned a lot. If I had to sum up a recurring message from all of them, in just a few words, that would be "We can be much better institutions, so that our communities can thrive."

In 1917, Eiichi went on a 18 day tour of the Hokuriku and Tohoku region, and addressed the communities. He declared following: "regional development is essential for the prosperity of the nation," "local action and effort are indispen-

序章 ● 渋沢栄一の"論語と算盤"の現代的意義は SDGs

sable for regional development," "the bank's progress relies on business prosperity."

It is clear that Eiichi Shibusawa's expectations for the regional communities and regional financial institution were very high. Even though the times are different, the expectations are the same, perhaps, higher.

Let's go.

第1章

普 遍 性
─時代を超えても大事なこと─

Chapter 1 ● Universality—Important
Things That Endure the Test of Time—

金融機関にとって唯一大事なものは「信用」

　SDGsの５つの原則で最初に掲げられているのは「普遍性」です。日本政府が提示した原則に示されているように、国内実施と国際協力の両面で率先して取り組むという「面」の側面もありますが、どの時代でも通じるという時間「軸」における普遍性も大事だと思います。

　特にサステナブルな世の中を求めるときには、変わらなければならないこともありますが、どの時代でも変わらないものの再確認も重要です。

　これから時代が変化するスピードは、どんどん速くなっていくでしょう。それは過去二十余年のコンピュータとインターネットの歴史を振り返ってもおわかりいただけると思います。1990年代の半ば、ようやくインターネットの商用サービスが開始され、「IT」という言葉が世に出始めた当時、二十数年後にはそれがIoTやICTへと発展し、携帯電話がスマートフォンという手の平サイズの高性能コンピュータになることを想像できた人は、世界を見渡してもほんの数名だったと思います。

　銀行がいままで顧客に提供していた金融サービスの「機能」は、これから店舗を介して提供する必要は技術的にはなく、ほぼスマートフォンにかわってしまうという将来が遠くありません。

　いま、50代半ばの人たちが国内系の銀行に就職した当時、恐らく周りからいわれたと思います。「これで定年まで安泰ですね」。

　そのくらい銀行という勤め先は安定した業種として知られていたのですが、それから30年、特に都市銀行を中心にして業界再編が進

TRUST is the most important asset

"Universality" is the first of the 5 Principles of the SDGs. The SDGs Promotion Headquarters of the Japanese Government defines "universality" as taking the lead both domestically and internationally for implementation. However, in addition to this geographic aspect of universality, another very important aspect is a sense of common values that remains consistent, during any era.

To achieve a sustainable world, somethings must change, but there are important things that endure the test of time.

The speed of change in our new era will only become faster and faster. Looking back over the past 20 years, computers and the internet changed our lives dramatically, where the mobile phone is now a communication device with high computing power, unimaginable several decades ago.

In order to deliver financial services to customers, at least from a technological point of view, all a bank needs is the smartphone, not branch offices.

When people in their mid-50s got their job at a Japanese bank about 3 decades ago, everybody probably thought that they were "all set until retirement." Nobody imagined back then that the industry would head towards an industry restructuring, where the 13 so-called "city banks" would be consolidated into 4 mega bank groups of today, Mitsubishi

みました。いまの若い銀行員からすれば、「都市銀行」という言葉自体が死語かもしれません。

　現在、メガバンクは三菱UFJフィナンシャル・グループ、三井住友フィナンシャルグループ、みずほフィナンシャルグループ、りそなホールディングスという4つの持ち株会社体制に移行していますが、30年ほど前は都市銀行だけで13行もありました。

　それが1990年に太陽神戸銀行と三井銀行が合併して「太陽神戸三井銀行」が誕生してから、徐々に都市銀行の再編が進み始め、1991年には協和銀行と埼玉銀行が合併して「協和埼玉銀行」になり、1996年には三菱銀行と東京銀行が合併して「東京三菱銀行」が誕生しました。そして、その後も業界再編はどんどん進み、現在のメガバンク4行体制になったのです。

　恐らく、1980年代の半ばあたりに就職活動をして都市銀行に入行した人たちは、まさか自分たちが業界再編のど真ん中に身を置くことになるなどとは、想像もしなかったと思います。

　一方、この30年間における地域金融機関の再編は、都市銀行と比べると比較的に限定的でした。いままでは。

　同じことがこれからの時代で通じると思う人は少ないでしょう。地域金融機関にお勤めの全員が、自分たちは業界再編のど真ん中に身を置くことになるという心構えが必要です。

　たまたまコンピュータと銀行を例にあげましたが、これからほうぼうで同じようなことが起こるでしょう。長いこと日本の経済を支えてきた自動車業界だって、内燃機関から電気自動車への移行を余儀なくされるおそれがあります。電気自動車になったら、いまのように複雑な内燃機関は不要になるので、自動車産業にとっては劇的な構造変化が起こるでしょう。あるいはAIの進化によって、いま

Financial Group, Mitsui Sumitomo Financial Group, Mizuho Financial Group, and Resona Holdings.

No one gaining employment at a large bank in the 1980's imagined that he would be caught in the middle of this massive restructuring of the industry.

On the other hand, the restructuring of regional financial institutions had been more limited. Until now.

Few people these days think that the ways of the past will continue into the future. Everybody working for a regional financial institution needs to be prepared to be in the middle of a major restructuring of the industry.

This disruptive change in industry is of course not just limited to the IT or finance, but destined for many other industries as well. Even the automotive industry, which has long supported Japan's economy, is being forced to shift from internal combustion engines to electric vehicles. This is a dramatic structural change for the industry.

It is said "ten years and a long time ago," but from now on, that may be "five years and a long time ago" or "three years and a long time ago."

Under these circumstances, it is imperative that a company must change for survival.

Yet, there is "universality" of things that is unchangeable despite the ever-changing business environment. Corporate philosophy of a company is one such example of universality.

はまだ存在している仕事のなかには、AIに取ってかわられて消え
ゆく運命のものもあります。

そういう意味では、地域金融だけが特別な存在とはいえません。

「十年ひと昔」などといいますが、これからは「五年ひと昔」あ
るいは「三年ひと昔」といわれる時代が来るかもしれません。

ただ、どれだけ世の中が大きく変わって、それに対応して変わら
なければならないことが多々あるとしても、変わらないものもあり
ます。いつの時代も、変わらずに必要とされる。これが「普遍性」
です。

多くの企業が「企業理念」を掲げていますが、この企業理念は普
遍性をもつもの、つまり50年、100年が経過したとしても変わらな
いものであることが大事です。

では、銀行にとって普遍的なものとは何でしょうか。それこそ渋
沢栄一が第一国立銀行を設立した当時からいまに至るまで、最も大
事とされる唯一無二のものが「信用」ではないでしょうか。

これは『論語と算盤』の「理想と迷信」という章のなかでも触れ
られています。

**「その経営せらるる事業に応じてよろしきを制して行くというこ
とは必要だろうと思うが、これを処するについて是非一つ守らなけ
ればならぬことは、前にも述べた商業道徳である。約すれば信の一
字である」**

つまり「信」の一文字を守ることができなければ、われわれ実業
界の基礎は強固とはいえないという意味です。

また、栄一は**「信用は実に資本であって　商売繁栄の根底であ
る」**（『渋沢栄一 訓言集』実業と経済）とも唱えています。会社経営
のためには資本が不可欠でありますが、それは「カネ」という財務

From this perspective, what is "universality" for banks?

If Eiichi Shibusawa were to have his say, he would probably say "Trust."

In *"Rongo and Soroban"*, Eiichi declares the following.

"It is important to manage the company according to the nature of the business. Yet, if there is one thing that must be obeyed at all times, that would be ethical conduct of business. And that, in one word, is Trust."

Eiichi believed **"Trust was indeed capital that is required to support prosperity of commerce,"** and capital is the very foundation of business.

Of course, financial capital is absolutely necessary for running a business, but if that company runs short of capital of "trust", then prosperity of the business is not sustainable.

In order to sustain prosperity for the society, financing for building social infrastructure is also crucial. However, having trust in social infrastructure, like trains arriving on time, salaries being paid properly, being sent by money transfers, etc. are normal here in Japan, but that isn't necessarily the case for some other countries.

In my conversations with top management at regional financial institutions as well as other industries, one thing that all of them value above all is "trust."

Sustainability is generally the most important goal for an organization, and profits of course are important to attain that sustainability. However, if making profits becomes the

的な資本だけではなく、信用という資本がなければ、そもそも会社の商売が継続することはありえません。

　また、国連が示したSDGsの5つのPの1つであるProsperity（繁栄）を支えるサステナブルな社会インフラを構築するためには、もちろん「カネ」が必要になります。一方、そのインフラに対する信用も不可欠でありましょう。電車が時刻どおりに運営され、給料日にはきちんと賃金が銀行を通して支払われ、送金できることなどは、日本で当たり前のことでありますが、そうではない国々が世界では少なくありません。

　地域金融機関のトップの方や、それ以外の企業経営者と話をしていても、つくづく実感させられるのですが、やはり民間の経済界に身を置いている人たちは、信用を何よりも重んじることを意識しています。本書を書くにあたって、お考えをお伺いした数名の地域金融機関の経営者、役員の多くが「銀行の生命は信用にある」と断言されていました。

　組織にとって持続性は一般に何よりも大事なことであり、その持続性のためには収益をあげることがもちろん大事です。ただ、収益確保だけを目的にしてしまうと、地域金融機関の理念から、どんどん離れてしまう懸念もあります。健全な収益確保は、あくまでも金融機関という組織を持続させるための手段であり、目的ではないのです。

大立志と小立志

　どの銀行も経営理念を掲げています。特に地域金融機関になる

sole objective, it is likely that the regional financial institutions will start drifting from their corporate philosophy that they hold dear. Healthy profit generation should be the means for sustainability, not the objective.

Big Goals and Small Goals ～～～～～

For regional financial institutions, these are the kind of

と、その経営理念のなかに、ほとんど必ず、「地域社会の発展を常に考える」「ふるさとの発展に役立つ」「地域社会の発展に寄与する」のような文言が入っています。

とても立派なことだと思います。

ただ、一つ気になることがあります。地域金融機関の現場で働いている人たちにとって、その経営理念が日々の具体的な仕事のやりがいにつながっているものであるか、ということです。

『論語と算盤』の「立志と学問」の章に、「大立志と小立志との調和」という項があり、そのなかに**「大なる立志と小さい立志と矛盾するようなことがあってはならぬ。この両者は常に調和し一致するを要するものである」**という言葉があります。

大なる立志とは、企業でいえば経営理念や創業の精神が該当します。前述した「地域社会の発展を常に考える」などというのが、地域金融機関にとっての大なる立志といってもよいでしょう。

これに対して小立志は、大なる立志を実現するための個々の目標、施策などを意味します。

そして、この大立志と小立志の間に矛盾が生じてはいけないと、栄一は述べています。

地域金融機関に就職してきた若手は、自分が生まれ育った地元に貢献したいという想いを強くもって入行したのだろうと思います。

ところが日々の小立志が、たとえば投資信託の販売ノルマが月1,000万円とか、今月の融資金額ノルマは4,000万円といった数値目標ばかりだったら、どうでしょう。それを達成できなければ早朝出勤、残業だらけということになって、上司から厳しく数字を詰められる。そうなると、お客様の意向はどうでもよいから、とにかく投資信託を売ってしまうとか、資金ニーズがない企業に無理をいって

words found in almost all their corporate philosophy.

"Always thinking about the development of the local community,"

"Being useful for the development of the hometown,"

"Contributing to the development of the local community."

This is very respectable. However, there is a question whether management philosophy like these is connected to the day-to-day job satisfaction for people working at the bank.

In *"Rongo and Soroban"*, Eiichi Shibusawa says:

"Big goals and small goals must not be in conflict. The two must always be in harmony and unified."

In the context of a company, "Big Goals" refer to such things as management philosophy and the spirit of founding the company.

On the other hand, "Small Goals" mean individual goals and measures to realize the "Big Goals. And, according to Eiichi, these two should not contradict each other.

Most young members join regional financial institutions because of their strong desire to contribute to the regional community where they were born and raised.

However, if they feel pressured by their superiors about reaching their monthly quota for commissions earned, they may have incentive to stuff their customers with funds or loans, regardless of needs.

This is a typical case where Big Goals and Small Goals

借入れをしてもらうとか、志が折れた行動に走る行員もいると思います。

　これは地域金融機関に限ったことではありません。たとえば証券会社でも、「日本の資本市場の発展に寄与する」という大立志があるにもかかわらず、支店の営業担当者が手数料収入のためにお客様を言いくるめて目先の利益というニンジンをぶら下げながら、リスクの本質がわかりづらい投資信託を販売するようなケースが見られたりします。

　まさに大立志と小立志が矛盾している典型例といってもよいでしょう。そして、これが日常的に行われるようになってしまうと、行員たちもどんどん疲弊してしまい、やがて銀行を辞めていくという事態に陥ってしまいます。

　したがって、普遍性として経営理念を掲げるのであれば、日々の行動と矛盾してはならないのです。

　そして、大立志と小立志が矛盾しないようにするためには、銀行の本店と支店の間の意思伝達や意識の壁など組織運営の見直しも必要になります。

　経営陣を含む本部の役割は、支店も含めた組織全体のマネジメントであり、経営方針や経営計画を策定し、その計画を達成するために、各支店の力量に応じて販売目標などを決定します。ただ、ここでありがちなパターンが、本部としては無用のトラブルを避けたいので支店に対して「あまり無理はしないでください」といいつつも、実はかなり厳しい販売目標を設定しているということです。

　一方、現場としてはその厳しい販売目標を達成しなければ、自分たちの成績が落ちて将来の出世にかかわるおそれがあるので、厳しい販売目標設定であったとしても、何が何でも達成しようとします。

are in conflict. If this continues day-to-day, they get exhausted, and perhaps end up resigning.

To ensure that Big Goals and Small Goals do not contradict each other, it is important to recognize such problems within the organization's management norms. For instance, one important aspect is whether there are any "walls" of communication or awareness between the headquarters and branch offices.

The role of management and headquarters is to manage the entire organization, to formulate management policies, and to determine sales targets accordingly. However, headquarters wanting to avoid unnecessary trouble, may say, "Don't overdo it" to the branch, but at the same time say, "By the way, this is your sales target this month."

On the other hand, from the perspective of the branch, unless they achieve those sales targets, then they fear their performance and standing within the organization may fall, leading to negative effects in career advancement. So, they have incentive to achieve the allocated sales targets, using whatever the means possible.

This is just an example of the wall between the headquarters and the branches. No matter how eloquent the management philosophy is written, the full potential of the bank will not be realized.

However, there are some changes of tune from the top management of some regional financial institutions. "Head-

まさに本部と支店の間に意識の壁が存在する典型例といってもよいでしょう。このような壁がある組織は、いくら表向きは立派な経営理念を掲げていたとしても、その銀行が本来もっているポテンシャルを発揮できずに終わってしまいます。

　ただ、このような問題点を直視し、組織のポテンシャルを引き出そうとしている地域金融機関の経営トップもいらっしゃいます。

　「本部は指示するところではなく、現場の要望を叶えるところだ」

　確たるメッセージをもつトップの存在感の重要性は、パーパスある組織の普遍性であります。

　地域金融機関が経営理念をもって組織に普遍性を与えるためには、経営も、本店も、そして支店も、同じ理念を共有できるように、大立志と小立志が矛盾をきたさないような組織運営がきわめて重要です。

　SDGsにおける大立志は「誰一人取り残さない」であります。大立志は、スローガンではなく、まさに理念です。そして、その理念を果たすために、17のゴール、169のターゲット、232の指標という小立志が設けられています。ここで、もちろん渋沢栄一が指摘しているように大立志と小立志は矛盾してはなりません。

　またSDGsの観点から大立志・小立志を考えると、一つ重要な思考回路が見えてきます。小立志の積み重ねで大立志を達成することではない、ということです。

　SDGsの文脈で「ムーンショット」という表現が使われます。「遠い月に打つ」というように、現在では仮に現実味がなくても大立志へと飛躍する。そして、その大立志を達成している将来からバックキャスト（逆算）しながら小立志を設けるという考え方です。

　「発展している豊かな地域社会」という大立志から、バックキャ

quarters are not to send down orders, but rather to give a place to meet the needs of the field."

The strong presence of top management is a universality of any organization with purpose.

"No one left behind" is the Big Goal for the SDGs. It is not merely a slogan, but rather an expression for universality. That is why in order to achieve this Big Goal, the Smaller Goals of 17 goals, 169 targets, and 232 indicators were also determined. As Eiichi Shibusawa demanded, these Small Goals are not contradictory to the Big Goal.

An important way to think about SDGs is that the Big Goal "No one left behind" is not there to be achieved as the result of adding up the Smaller Goals. Rather, as the phrase "moonshot" indicates, determining the Big Goal comes first, and the Smaller Goals are derived through back-casting.

So, if the Big Goal for the regional financial institution is "The development of well-being for the regional community," this should come first, and the day-to-day Small Goals are determined from back-casting. If those who work at regional financial institutions feel that these Small Goals, day-to-day tasks, are inconsistent with the Big Goal, then you can be sure that Eiichi would demand to improve that condition immediately.

ストする小立志が、地域金融機関の行員の日々の業務と矛盾しているのであれば、直ちに改善せよ、と渋沢栄一は喝を入れることでしょう。

普遍性で大事な「と」の力 〜〜〜〜〜

　私の持論ですが、普遍性を考えるうえで大事なのは「と」の力だと思っています。

　"論語と算盤"は、道徳を意味する論語と、商売を意味する算盤を、「論語か算盤」という二項対立ではなく、本来なら相反するものを、「と」の力で融合させ化学反応を引き起こすところに要諦があります。

　地域金融機関のなかでも地方銀行になると、その多くが株式を上場しています。すると、地域貢献か株主かの二項対立に陥りがちです。採算性は二の次で少しでも地元経済の発展のために尽くしたいという想いがある一方で、株式を上場している以上は利益の最大化を求める株主がいるため、収益を重視したビジネスをせざるをえない。地元貢献か株主かの選択を強いられるのです。

　たしかに、地域貢献と株主は一見すると対立する存在なのかもしれません。でも、そこを対立させることなく、地域貢献と株主の利益を両立させる方法を考えるのが経営です。

　どうすればよいのか。具体的な答えがあるわけではありませんが、一つ提案したいのは、地元経済圏のなかだけで物事を完結させると思わないことです。地域金融機関が、ビジネスの基盤を置いている地元にいる中小企業、あるいは個人への貸付や預貯金、あるい

The power of "and" for universality

The power of "and," which is the essence of *"Rongo and Soroban"*, is crucial for universality.

RONGO and SOROBAN is a paradigm that these believes (morality and business) are not dichotomies. The two need to be integrated in order to bring about a "chemical reaction" to create value.

Many regional banks are listed as public companies. This often puts them in a difficult position because serving the regional community and maximizing profits for shareholders may be seen as contradictory.

Certainly, it may be a difficult situation, but it is the role of management to find ways so that these two important stakeholders' interests are in fact aligned.

Perhaps one way is to look for answers outside boundaries of the local economy, not just within.

It is natural for regional financial institutions to have their eyes set on their local communities. However, in a rapidly aging society, near sightedness may hinder seeing that the traditional way to doing business is not sustainable.

は最近だと資産運用などで商売をしようと思うのは自然なことです。これが、同機関のパーパス、存在意義であることに間違いありません。

　ただ高齢少子化社会が加速する現状において近視眼的な視野に陥ると、従来のビジネスモデルだけでは持続可能でないことが見えてこないという課題が多く残されてしまいます。

　したがって、視野を広めて地元経済とともに新しいフロンティアも求める必要があります。しかし、日本国内の大都市圏に進出しても、そこにはすでにメガバンクなど強豪がたくさんありますから、そこで競争しても敵うわけがありません。

　だからこそ世界を見据えるのです。といっても、海外のメジャーなグローバル金融機関と競争しろというわけではありません。地域金融機関には地域金融機関なりのローカルな方法で、グローバルに闘う方法があるはずです。海外事業にすでに進出している、あるいは進出を模索している地元企業の数は、地域で少なくないと思います。

　ローカルとグローバル。この「と」の力を実現させることができれば、まさに地域創出という新しいクリエイションが生じます。

　東京や都市圏を介することなく、地元企業と世界を直接につなげることによって収益をあげれば、地域貢献と株主の両方を満足させることが可能になるはずです。かつて都市圏に行かなければ情報がなかった時代がありました。現在はインターネット等を通じて、日本国内のどの地域であっても、世界の情報・情勢をキャッチすることができます。

　さまざまな情報コミュニケーションの手段はすでに存在していますので、残るはマインドのリセットだけです。

There is a need to expand the vision beyond for new frontiers. Yet, the big cities in Japan are already crowded markets, and the competition is tough.

That is why it is important for regional financial institutions to expand horizons globally as well. This does not mean competing with the major global players in the world, but rather, identifying companies in the regional community that already have extended or is thinking about extending their businesses globally.

Local and global. If this power of "and" is realized, this is value creation that will vitalize the regional community.

With advances in information technologies available these days, there is no need to come through Tokyo or other big cities. You can go direct to new markets abroad. If regional financial institutions can assist local businesses to identify these new markets, then it would be possible to satisfy both the local community as well as the shareholders.

The means are already available now more than ever as mentioned above. Only thing that remains is change of mindset.

At a time when Japan was on the path of rapid economic growth during the Showa Era, Japanese automakers and electronic manufacturers were able to satisfy the mass consumption demands, mostly from advanced economies like the US, with exports high quality mass production. "Made in Japan" swept the world.

日本が高度経済成長の道を突き進んでいた当時、日本の自動車メーカーや家電メーカーは、日本国内で製造した製品を、米国をはじめとする主に先進国の、大量消費の需要を満たす大量生産の輸出で外貨を稼いできました。「メイド・イン・ジャパン」が世界を席巻したのです。

　それがあまりにも成功したため、米国をはじめとする諸外国からジャパン・バッシングを受けるようになりました。貿易不均衡を是正するため、輸出数量制限を受けるのと同時に、日本が海外からより多くのモノを輸入するように、各種輸入自由化が行われました。

　そんなことを行っているうちに時代は平成になり、日本の人口動態がピラミッド型からひょうたん型に移っていきました。いままでの日本経済の高度成長の主役であった団塊世代の高齢化が進み、彼らの子ども世代である団塊ジュニアは就職氷河期と景気低迷にもまれます。海外のように日本では潰れることはないと思われていた銀行の倒産、経営統合が相次いだ時代でもあります。

　一方、バッシングを回避し、海外に製造拠点を移すことによって海外各国の雇用創出に寄与し、貿易不均衡に対する攻撃の矛先をかわすねらいもあり、日本のメーカーは生産拠点を海外に移転させました。海外で製造しても製造元は日本メーカーという製品が、世界中に出回るようになりました。つまり、昭和時代のメイド・イン・ジャパンから平成時代のメイド・バイ・ジャパンに移行していったのです。ただ、ジャパン・バッシングで始まった平成時代は、日本が素通りされたジャパン・パッシングの時代でもありました。

　そして、現在は令和時代に入ったわけですが、断言します。日本はきわめて重要な時代の節目に立っています。

　これから日本の人口動態がひょうたん型から一気に逆ピラミッド

It was so successful that Japan started to receive "bashing" from the US and other countries. In order to decrease trade imbalances, import liberalization and export volume restrictions were enacted.

Meanwhile, Japan entered the Heisei Era from 1989, and the demographics of Japan moved from the population pyramid shape to the double barbel shape, the aging baby boomer generation and the boomer junior generation.

By moving manufacturing overseas to avoid the "bashing," Japan modified the "Made in Japan" model to "Made by Japan" in your country model. The Heisei Era started out with "bashing," but became to be known for Japan "passing."

Japan entered the new Reiwa Era in 2019. This also coincides with the beginnings of a critical juncture for a new society for Japan.

The demographics of Japan will shift quite dramatically from the double-barreled shaped Heisei Era to an inverted-pyramid shaped Reiwa Era, a generational shift at a speed and scale that Japanese society has never experienced before.

With such a dramatic demographic shift rapidly accelerating, a new model for Japan is essential. Not just relying on the "Made in Japan" successes of the Showa Era or the "Made by Japan" of the Heisei Era, but rather, "Made with Japan." This is the new model for the Reiwa Era, where Ja-

型に移行します。つまり、高齢者人口がどんどん増える一方、若年層人口が一向に増えず、逆三角形の人口分布になっていくのです。つまり、いままで日本社会が見たことがなかったスピード感と規模の世代交代が始まっているのです。

　つまり、いままでの成功体験をつくってくださった世代から、これからの時代に新たな成功体験を築かなければならない世代への壮大なバトンタッチです。

　日本全体が、このような時代を迎えることになりますが、地域差も生じてくるでしょう。限界集落とはいかないまでも、若者がどんどん大都市圏に移り住むようになり、年老いた親世代が地元に残されているような地域は、人口動態の逆ピラミッド型が一気に進むおそれがあります。

　そのような時代が到来するなかで、昭和時代の「メイド・イン・ジャパン」の成功体験だけではなく、平成時代の「メイド・バイ・ジャパン」だけでもなく、これからの令和時代の日本は、「メイド・ウィズ・ジャパン」を目指すべきだと思います。日本が持続可能に繁栄する社会を世界と共創していく新しい時代の新しい成功体験です。

　こうした日本からの「メイド・ウィズ・ジャパン」の呼びかけに世界で数多い新興国や発展途上国は、好感を示してくれるのではないでしょうか。

　アジアではインド、インドネシアやベトナム、ミャンマー、カンボジアなど、そして、アフリカ大陸の国々で過半数を占めている国民は、20代、30代の若い世代です。日本とは異なりピラミッド型の人口動態をもっており、この社会構造から今後は経済的に大きな発展が期待できます。

pan co-creates prosperity and sustainability with the world.

This new model for Japan will likely be especially welcomed by the emerging and developing countries in the world. In many countries in Asia, such as India, Indonesia, Vietnam, Myanmar, Cambodia, India, and countries of the African continent, the population is still young. Unlike Japan, their population demographics are still pyramid shaped, and as such, potential for great economic growth.

However, what are the young people in these countries looking for? Getting work, earning income, and supporting their family. Things taken for granted in Japan.

At the same time, emerging and developing countries face many social challenges. That is the reason for the SDGs, and why Japan should be involved in achieving these goals.

Japan has the capability for the finding solutions that can improve the lives of many people, in many countries. This is not limited to just large Japanese companies, but also small and medium-sized enterprises, startups, not only in big cities but also in regional communities.

If the many people of many countries of the world feel that Japan is necessary for their well-being, Japan will be a necessary partner in their livelihoods. If Japan is needed by the world in this manner, even if the population inside the borders of Japan is declining, an era of prosperity is definitely possible.

This is "Made with Japan," for the new era, by a new gen-

こうした国々の若手が求めているのは何でしょう。それは仕事に就いて、収入を得て家族を養うということです。いずれも日本では当たり前と思われていることです。そこにかなりの成長の伸びしろがあります。

　ただ、新興国や発展途上国の場合、成長の可能性があるものの多くの社会的課題も抱えています。だから、SDGsなのです。先進国では当たり前と思われている多くのことが新興国や発展途上国では実現できていないのです。

　そこに日本は大企業だけではなく、中堅、中小、スタートアップまで、都市圏だけではなく、もちろん地方まで、いろいろな側面で、多くの国々の大勢の人々の生活を向上させる解決策をもっているはずです。

　世界の多くの国々の、大勢の人々から、日本は自分たちの生活に必要なパートナーなんだという状態が実現できれば、どうでしょう。日本国土内の人口が減ったとしても、そこに彼らの持続的な成長の恩恵が還元され、繁栄の時代を築けるのではないでしょうか。

　これが「メイド・ウィズ・ジャパン」が目指す、新たな時代の、新たな世代の、新たな価値観による成功体験です。

　このように新しい成功体験を築くことが、日本におけるSDGs、持続可能な開発の目標です。地域創生は重要で、否定すべきではまったくありません。ただ、SDGsバッジを付けることが「サステナブル・イン・ローカル」という次元だけでお考えであれば、それはSDGが掲げている本質ではありません。

　重要なのは、あくまでも「ウィズ」です。「ローカル・ウィズ・グローバル」「サステナブル・ウィズ・ジャパン」「メイド・ウィズ・ジャパン」。これが、SDGsバッジを付ける意味の本質であり

eration, co-creating prosperity with new common values.

This is why the SDGs are important in the context of Japan. Revitalization of the regional community is very important. However, the SDGs badge does not represent "sustainability in local," but rather, is stressing the importance of "with" the world.

"Local with Global," "Sustainability with Japan," "Made with Japan." This is the essence for wearing the SDG badge.

Eiichi Shibusawa declared, "**Economy has no borders. We must proceed with our wisdom and determination in all directions.**"

He also observed, "**If you gaze from the heavens to mankind, they are all created equal. The people of the Four seas are all brothers, so it is our duty to be kind and caring for others, provide food, clothing, and shelter.**"

In regional communities of Japan, there are companies that agree with this sense of purpose and want to expand their business this way. However, they perhaps lack the human resources, network and financing. That is where the regional financial institutions should step in to provide support and assistance.

"Supporting the various stages of a customer."

"Creating added value of others."

"Ability to foresee the future and provide."

These are kind of talk that I heard from top management

ます。

　渋沢栄一は「経済に国境なし。いずれの方面においても、わが智恵と勉強とをもって進むことを主義としなければならない」（『渋沢栄一　訓言集』国家と社会）といいました。

　また「天より人を視れば、みな同じく生みしところのものである。ゆえに四海の人々はみな兄弟であるから、人々相親しみ、相愛して、衣食住を営むは、天に対する務めである」（『渋沢栄一　訓言集』道徳と功利）とも唱えています。

　日本の地域社会において、このような想いに賛同し、事業を通じて応えられる企業は必ず存在しています。このパーパスに意義を感じて事業展開したいと考えているはずです。地域に密着する金融機関として、これら企業を発掘し、金融的・人的・ネットワーク的に彼らのパーパスの実現を支援することが、自分たち自身のパーパスでもあるはずです。

　「お客様のさまざまのステージを支えること」

　「相手の付加価値をつくる」

　「これからどういうことが起こるか推察して提案する力」

　このような想いが、地域金融機関の経営トップから聞こえてきます。まさに地域社会に新しい価値を共創する「と」の力といってもよいでしょう。

「普遍性」からみた地域金融機関のあり方

　地域金融機関のパーパスは、主に地元経済を活性化させるために金融サービスを提供することです。これはまさにすべての地域金融

of regional financial institutions. This is the power of "and," to co-create new value for the regional communities.

Perspective of "universality" for regional financial institutions ～～～

Regional financial institutions' purpose of existence is to provide financial services as to vitalize the local economy.

機関にとって普遍的なことといってよいでしょう。多くの地域金融機関が経営理念に「地域社会の発展を常に考える」ということを理念として掲げています。

渋沢栄一は決して、道徳と殖利が矛盾するものだとは考えていませんでした。つまり、地域金融機関にとって地域の発展に貢献することと収益の追求はまったく矛盾しないということになります。

最近、「インパクト投資」という言葉を目にする機会が増えました。これは、本業を通じて社会的な課題の解決に取り組んでいる企業などに投資することによって、社会的なリターンと経済的なリターンの両立を目指すことです。まさに、現代的"論語と算盤"です。

ただ、企業が事業の経済的活動を正当化するために社会的課題への取組みをアピールするという、「ウォッシング」、いわば「お化粧」の課題がありがちです。ファンド業界でも同じような課題があります。「インパクト投資」は響きがよい言葉であり、また、人によって定義が異なる傾向があります。

真のインパクト投資にはきちんとした定義があります。社会的課題の解決に取り組むことを意図として、その事業がきちんと持続できるように経済的なリターンを求めるという投資です。つまり、「意図」がどこに置かれているかがポイントです。「おまけ」ではないのです。

これは、これから積極的に地域金融機関が開発すべき投資のフロンティアではないでしょうか。地域のさまざまな社会的課題に取り組む手段として、現在、世界において新しい時代の投資手法として脚光を浴びているインパクト投資の可能性について、真剣に取り組むべきです。

This is the universality for all regional financial institutions, and therefore, is expressed as such in their corporate philosophy.

Eiichi Shibusawa never considered morality and profit-making to be contradictory with one another. Therefore, it is fair to say that, for regional financial institutions, contributing to the development of their community and pursuing profits do not contradict each other.

The word "impact investment" is starting to get more and more acknowledgement recently. This is a type of investment that pursues both social impact as well as economic returns by investing in companies that strives to solve social issues through business solutions. It is the modern day RONGO and SOROBAN in action.

However, some companies try to justify their economic activities to public, by so-called "washing," to make it appear as though they are engaged in social issues. This problem is also prevalent in the fund investment industry as well, because the word "impact investment" sounds very appealing. Therefore, it has a tendency to mean different things to different people.

True impact investment has a clear definition. The intent of impact investment is positive impact. In other words, finding solutions for social issues. But for that impact to be sustainable, it requires economic returns.

In this respect, impact investment is a new frontier that the

ただ、ここで組織的なハードルになるのが、恐らく「投資」という部分でしょう。特に地域金融機関は、預貯金を通じて集めた資金で企業向け貸出することが伝統的な事業であり、価格変動（リスク）ある投資には不慣れな傾向があります。

　ところが地方経済が力を失っていくにつれて、企業向け貸出が伸びなくなりました。その分を国債の運用に回して補っていましたが、債券と比べると変動リスクが高いエクイティ（株式）に資金を投入する投資経験やマインドセットが豊富とはいえません。そもそも自己資本に対するリスク資産比率の規制が設けられています。

　ただ、地域社会の投資銀行になることが、地域金融機関の一つの生き残りの策になるでしょう。

　これはちょっと言葉遊びのようになるので恐縮ですが、とはいえ恐らくかなり真実を突いていると思います。「投資」という漢字から受けるイメージは、どこかに「資」金を「投」げるという感じがあると思います。結果、自分たちの地域からお金が外部に流れてしまうという誤解を生んでいると思います。

　ただ「投資」を漢字ではなく英語で考えてみてください。英語で投資を「Invest」といいます。「In」は入れる。「vest」はチョッキのことですね。この２つが組み合わさって「Invest」になるわけです。これが意味するところは、自分の生活圏の外のさまざまなところにある成長の可能性を取り込むことができるチケットのようなものがあって、それを自分が着ているベストのポケットに入れておくということです。

　日本の地方には、地域金融機関の預貯金を通じて多額のお金が眠っています。その一部は各地域金融機関の地元企業への融資というかたちで還元されていますが、地方銀行の預貸率は、一部を除く

regional financial institutions should definitely develop. Impact investing is a new emerging global trend, and the regional community and financial institutions should be a part of it.

However, there is probably an institutional hurdle regarding "investment." The traditional business for regional financial institutions have been collecting deposits and lending to companies to earn an interest rate spread. In general, regional financial instutions are not used to investing assets with fluctuating price risk.

With regional economies slowing down along with loan demand, regional financial institutions have been actively investing in government bonds, but in general, their expertise and mindset has been generally limited regarding equity investments, which has higher price risk compared to bonds.

However, the word "invest" is "in"+"vest." What are we putting "in" our "vest"? Well, sort of a ticket. A ticket that allows you to bring in growth from outside the borders of your community, and you put that "in" your "vest."

This is the essence of "invest," and it is not about throwing your money, as the Kanji characters "tou-shi" (investment) in the Japanese language would indicate.

In the regional communities throughout Japan, large amounts of cash are sleeping in deposits. Some of this money circulates in the community in the form of loans to companies. However, the loan to deposit ratio for most regional

と100％を下回っています。50％台のところもあります。預金を通じてお金を集めて、貸し出すことによって利鞘を得るというビジネスモデルは、すでに厳しい状況にあるということです。

　だからこそ、地域金融機関も一歩踏み出して投資を検討する必要があります。それも、いたずらにハイリスク・ハイリターンを追求するような投資ではなく、前述したようなインパクト投資も自己資金のポートフォリオの一環として積極的に視野に入れるべきでしょう。

　地域社会における、これからの「インパクト」に間違いなく、日本政府の「2050年カーボンニュートラル宣言」があるでしょう。そして、その要になるのが再生可能エネルギーの発展です。

　北海道の十勝高原の北方にある上士幌町とご縁をいただいていますが、食糧自給率が3,000％という驚異的な地域です。再生可能エネルギーの自給率が1,090％もあり、その大半は水力発電ですがバイオマス発電だけでも100％の電力需要を満たすことができるようです。

　日本全国の自治体が上士幌町のようにはなれないことは、明らかです。ただ、2050年までにカーボンニュートラルを目指すことが既定路線になったことから、それに関連する事業を発展させなければなりません。「日本は検討や調整などで意思決定に時間がかかる、けれども、いったん、目標が決定したら、必ずそれを成し遂げる」と長年、日本人は自己評価していました。さて、目標が決定されました。それを、われわれ日本人は成し遂げなければなりません。

　このような地域社会のインパクトに資金や経営支援を提供しながら経済的リターンを目指すことは、地域金融機関の一つのあり方だと思います。大きな時代の流れになることに間違いないカーボン

financial institutions are below 100%, some even below 50%.

The reasons why regional financial institutions should also engage in investment are clear. Of course, reckless investment in high risk – high return financial instruments must be avoided. Yet, including impact investment as a part of their portfolio makes good sense for regional financial institutions.

One obvious potential for "impact" for the regional communities is the "2050 Carbon Neutral" declaration by the Japanese Government. Renewable energy capabilities will definitely be an important area for development.

In Kamishihoro Town in the northern part of Tokachi, Hokkaido, the self-sufficiency rate for food product is an astonishing 3,000%, and the self-sufficiency rate of renewable energy is as high as 1,090%. Most of this energy is in the form of hydropower, but biomass power generation alone is 100%.

Of course, not all regional communities can be like Kamishihoro. However, because the 2050 carbon neutral target has been made clear, related businesses and projects must be developed. Japan has long been saying, "It takes time for Japan to make a decision, but once the decision is made, it gets done." Well, the decision was made. Japan has to get it done.

Making available the funds and assistance to get this done

ニュートラルを地域産業の新しい成長戦略として実現させること
は、地域金融機関にとっての普遍的な価値＝信用を創出することと
直につながります。

　現状を維持することに満足することなく、将来を見据え、その未
来を地域とともに拓くことが、密着型金融機関の普遍性あるパーパ
スそのものです。

　渋沢栄一は『青淵百話』という講演集で「会社銀行員の必要的資
格」という考えを助言しています。

　第一　実直になること。

　第二　勤勉精励なること。

　第三　着実なること。

　第四　活潑になること。

　第五　温良なること。

　第六　規律を重んずること。

　第七　耐忍力あること。

　すべて、社会と密着している金融機関であるからこそ重要な普遍
性ある要素です。地域社会におけるインパクトの担い手になるの
は、地域金融機関のほか、誰がいるのでしょうか。

in their communities is an important role for regional financial institutions. The big megatrend of carbon neutral must be a growth strategy for both of them, it will be their calling to provide their universality, which is trust.

Not being complacent with the status quo, foreseeing the future and co-creating the future with their community. This is the regional financial institutions' universality, its purpose.

Eiichi Shibusawa left some advice in a speech titled "The Necessary Qualifications for Bankers."

First, be honest.

Second, be diligent and industrious.

Third, be stable.

Fourth, be engaged.

Fifth, be amiable.

Sixth, be disciplined.

Seventh, be resilient.

All very important elements of universality for regional financial institutions serving their communities. Who else other than them can provide the kind of impact that is necessary for their communities ?

第2章

包 摂 性
―誰一人取り残さない社会へ―

Chapter 2 ● Inclusiveness
― Society of No One Left Behind ―

Me から We へ、We から Me へ の循環をつくる

　包摂性、「誰一人取り残さない」は、SDGs という大立志そのものです。このような社会を、地域内ではもちろんのこと、地域外の世の中でもつくることが SDGs の精神です。

　ただ、精神論だけでは何も解決することができません。おカネが必要です。SDGs を達成するためには、年間2.5兆ドルが必要であるとよくいわれています。ちなみに、これは途上国・新興国向けだけで先進国の課題解決を含まず、**かつ**、ビフォーコロナの金額です。

　莫大な金額で、政府予算や伝統的な援助資金だけでは SDGs に到達できないということが明らかであり、新たなおカネの流れをつくることが必要です。さて、どうする？

　世の中に理財に長じる人たちが必要です。それも少数精鋭ではなく、世の中で大人数が。それでは、「理財に長じる人」とは、どのような存在でしょうか。

　「真に理財に長じる人は、よく集むると同時によく散ずるようでなくてはならぬ」（『論語と算盤』「能く集め能く散ぜよ」）という言葉を渋沢栄一は残しています。

　ここでいう「よく散ずる」は、気ままに乱費するという意味ではもちろんありません。世の中に資金をよく還元する「We のお金の使い方」を指しています。「Me」のためだけではなく。

　では、この「We のお金の使い方」とは何でしょうか。

　私は2008年に同志らとコモンズ投信という「世代を超える投資」を目指す投資信託会社を設立しました。多くの地域金融機関から、

Creating a Cycle of from Me to We and from We to Me ~~~~~~~~

Inclusiveness, as defined by "No one left behind," is the very ideal of the great ambitions of mankind that gave birth to the SDGs. The spirit of the SDGs is to create a society that achieves this ideal not only in the regional community, but also in the world.

However, idealism alone cannot deliver the solutions. You need money. It is often cited that $ 2.5 trillion per year is needed to achieve the SDGs. And, this astronomical amount of money is needed for emerging and newly developed countries, and does not include solutions for the developed countries, AND, it is before the Covid-19 global crisis.

It is clear that the SDGs cannot be achieved with government budgets and traditional aid funding alone. Creation of new flow of money is necessary.

Therefore, it is obvious that our world needs people who excel in finance, not only in the selected elite, but in the general population.

Eiichi Shibusawa observed the following, "**People who truly excel in finance must gather it well, and at the same time, spread it well.**"

Of course, "spread it well" does not mean spending money freely without care, but rather, recirculating the money back into society with intent. The concept of using money

私たちが運用するファンドを取り扱いいただいています。

　この運用会社を立ち上げた起源の2001年に、自分自身が親となって抱いていた小さな赤ちゃんが将来は成人となる、遠い未来を見つめていました。

　その時、親の元を離れ、新しいことにチャレンジしている成人となった子どもを応援する資金を毎月積み立てて投資していこうと思い立ったのです。当時ではきわめて Me、自分と自分の家族のためという出発点でした。

　子どもが自分の長期投資のきっかけをつくってくれたので、その後に仲間たちと立ち上げたコモンズ投信ではお子さん向けの「こどもトラスト」というプログラムを設けました。結果、会社設立来の直接販売の口座開設は 6 人のうちの 1 人が未成年、コロナ禍の直近ではおよそ 3 割、という実績は、恐らく運用業界では世界 No. 1 であると自負しています。

　長年、子どもと長期的に積み立てるお金について意識している資産運用会社なので、子ども向け、親子向けのセミナーを年間に数多く開催しています。この「コモンズこどもトラストセミナー」のシリーズで、子どもたちに「お金の使い方」を学ぶセミナーを繰り返したことから「We のお金の使い方」の気づきが芽生えました。

　物事はちょっとした発想の転換によってまったく違ったものになるということです。Me は私です。ミーイズムという考え方があって、これは自分の満足や幸せを求めるだけで、他にはいっさい関心を払わない考え方のことです。自己中心主義といってもよいでしょう。

　ところが、M の字を天地ひっくり返すと、W になります。Me から We へ。We は「私たち」です。

for "We," not just "Me."

In 2008, a group of colleagues and myself established Commons Asset Management, a mutual fund company that aims to deliver "investment across generations." Many regional financial institutions carry our fund as a part of the line-up for their customers.

The origin of our company started in 2001 when I became a parent, holding my baby son, and looking towards the distant future. Someday, this little baby will grow up, and will become an adult. At that time, he will likely be taking on some challenge in his life. So, to be prepared to support that future challenge, I decided to put a little bit of money aside every month and make long term investments in his name.

Because of these origins, preparing for the next generation, Commons Asset Management created a program called "Kodomo (Child) Trust." As a result, currently after 12 years since inception, 1 out of 6 established accounts are minors, 1 out of 3 during the current Covid Crisis.

Because we have a special focus of long term investment for the next generation, we frequently provide seminars for kids and their parents. Through my experience as a speaker at these seminars, I discovered this revelation regarding "Me" and "We."

If you flipflop "M", it turns into a "W". Thus, the conceptual origins of using money from "Me" to "We" was born.

When we talk to the kids, we teach them four ways about

これをお金の使い方に当てはめると、Me のお金の使い方は、もっぱら自分の満足、自分の幸せのための使い方です。

　これに対して We のお金の使い方は、自分と自分が所属しているコミュニティ全体が豊かになるための使い方になります。最近、関心が高まっている、ウェルビーイングのためのお金の使い方が、「We のお金の使い方」といってもよいでしょう。

　具体的には、コモンズこどもトラストセミナーで「お金の使い方」については、以下の4つの展開になります。

　1つ目のお金の使い方は、どんなに小さい子どもでもわかることで、文字どおり「使う」ことです。コンビニエンスストアなどに行って、商品棚に自分が食べたいお菓子があったら、お金を払ってそれを買う。お金の最も身近な使い方であって、ほとんどの子どもたちが理解できます。

　2つ目は「貯める」ことです。自分のほしいものが、たとえばゲームソフトのように少し値の張るものであった場合、自分の手持ちのお金で足りなければ、お小遣いを貯めて買えます。

　この2つのお金の使い方は小さなお子さんでもすぐわかってくれることです。なぜなら、それは自分のことだから。つまり「Me のお金の使い方」です。

　そこで3つ目のお金の使い方になるのですが、これはほとんどのお子さんが日常的に触れるお金の使い方ではないでしょう。しかし、丁寧にお話すれば必ずわかってくれます。なぜなら、お子さんでもしっかりとした良心をもっているからです。

　「寄付」というお金の使い方です。

　たとえば遠くに困っている人がいるとします。お子さんに助けてあげたいという良心が働きます。ただ自分はまだ子どもだから、そ

using money.

The first is an easy concept for kids to understand, "spend." If you want candy at a store you need to spend money to get it.

The second is also relatively easy to understand as well. If a child wants to buy a game software, they probably do not have enough money to do so. So, we teach them about "save."

These two ways of using money, "spend" and "save" are relatively easy for kids to understand, because it is about themselves, or "Me."

The third is probably a little bit more difficult for kids to understand, because for most of them, this use of money is likely not in their daily routine. But, when we explain to them carefully, they definitely understand.

They understand because even little kids have compassion. The third way to use money is to "donate."

When someone is in need, even little kids want to help. However, they are children. "I can't go all by myself to somewhere to help people, and even if I could go there, I won't be of much use." Their faces cloud, when they realize that they cannot do anything to help.

However, as they listen to our talk, they start to see it. "I can't go myself, but there are others that can go to help. If I donate a little bit of money from my savings, with my friends, family and other people, then they can go to help

んなに遠くまで一人で出かけて困っている人たちの手助けをすることができない。行けたとしても、自分は子どもだから力があまりない。自分は何もできない。困っている人がいるのに。

この現実の壁にぶつかったお子さんたちの顔が曇ります。

でも、説明を続けるとお子さんたちは気づきます。自分は助けに行けない。けれどもかわりに助けに行ける人たちがいる。その人たちが行けるように自分はお小遣いを少し使って「寄付」すればいいんだ！　と。

もちろん自分が寄付できる程度のお金では、まったく足りません。だから、自分だけでなく自分のお友達や家族など、周りの人たちにも少しずつお金を出してもらい、その人たちと一緒に寄付すれば、遠くにいて困っている人たちを助けることができる！

このお金の使い方がわかった子どもたちの顔は、今度はパッと明るくなります。そうか！　自分一人では何もできないけど、皆と一緒であればできるんだという気づきとめぐりあうことができたからです。

先ほど示したように、Mがひっくり返ってWになった瞬間です。Weのお金の使い方です。つまり「Weのお金の使い方」とは、社会課題を解決するために皆と一緒に実行するお金の使い方です。

このように、お金の使い方をMe視点からWe視点に変えることによって、SDGsでいうところのサステナブルな未来を築いていく理財が生じるわけです。一人ひとりの良心から。

さて、「Weのお金の使い方」にはもう1つあります。それは4つ目のお金の使い方である「投資」です。

日本人のなかには、投資というとあぶく銭を稼いでいるだけというネガティブなイメージがつきまといます。「ナンボ儲かるの」と

out where the need is!"

The kid's faces start to light up now. That is because kids realize that they are not, in fact, powerless. I can get things done, with others, towards a common cause.

This is the point where the kids figure it out, using money from "Me" to "We."

The fourth way to use money is "invest."

Of course, we could start with "invest," but, in doing so, the focus may be on how much money was made for "Me."

With the foundation of the concept for using money for "We," the narrative for kids can continue as follows.

In society, there are lot of companies that provides goods and services that bring value to their customers. The customer says "Oh, this is very good, thank you," and purchases the goods or services and pays money to the company. Receiving the money, the company says "thank you."

At the company, there is a lot of adults, much like their parents, working very hard. The company says, "Thank you for your work, here is your salary." The adults, in turn, "Thank you" too and receive the salary.

"So, that is why we kids have a meal on the table every night, have clothes to wear, and get to go on trips with the family!" The children can see that money is something that circulates in society, and eventually comes around to them for benefit.

And there is something else. Money that is circulates in

いう思いきり「Me」の次元の話になりそうです。

　ただ、たとえば、「Weのお金の使い方」を理解したお子さんに対してこのような話を展開できます。

　世の中には、お客さんの役に立つ商品やサービスを提供しているすてきな会社がたくさんあります。その商品やサービスを買っているお客さんたちは、「これがあって助かる。どうもありがとう」といって代金を払います。そして会社はお金を支払ってくれたお客さんに対して「ありがとうございます」と感謝の気持ちを示します。

　さらに、その会社には大勢の大人たち社員が働いています。お子さんたちから見れば自分のお父さんやお母さんのような大人たちです。会社は働いてくれている大人たちに「お疲れ様。どうもありがとう」といって、お給料を支払います。そして、大人たちは「どうもありがとうございました」といって、お給料を受け取ります。

　だから、自分たち子どもは、毎晩お食事をすることができて、服を買ってもらい、楽しい家族旅行に行けるんだ。

　このようにお金とは社会でめぐり回って流れてくるものだということが、お子さんの目に浮かんでくると思います。

　このようにお金は社会に循環しているということに加え、そこに必ず存在しているものがあります。それは「ありがとう」です。

　実は「ありがとう」の連鎖によってお金は社会にめぐり回り、経済活動は成り立っている。そして、その「ありがとう」が増えれば喜びが増える、喜びが増えれば増えるほど価値が高まる。実は「投資」とは「ありがとう」が増えることの応援なんだ、とお子さんにお話ができます。投資という「Weのお金の使い方」です。

　もちろん、これは小さなお子さん向けの話です。しかし、「ありがとう」の連鎖によって経済社会が成り立っている、その「ありが

society is always accompanied by a "thank you."

Therefore, "invest" is all about cheering the accumulation of these "thank you's." Investing, is in fact, using money for "We."

Of course, this story is for little kids. However, there is an essence here about using money that even adults should understand.

For instance, investing in companies that are promoting the achievement of a carbon neutral world or revitalizing in regional regions is a way to use money for "We."

This concept can be extended to consumption as well, such as purchasing clothing that is conscious about impact on the environment or production of chocolate that is free of child labor. Ethical consumption is also a way to use money for "We."

However, there are always people that just looks after their own benefits, or "Me." Yet, human beings are not solitary creatures and belong to some community or another. If you are only looking after for the benefit of "Me," is that really a life of prosperity and well-being? Is such a person wanted in the community?

We felt it firsthand with the Covid-19 crisis. It was very important to look after "Me" and the family. However, if "We" the society gets segregated and activities stops, "Me" cannot do anything. It is only when "We" is working properly that "Me" can carry on with a prosperous life of

とう」が増えることの応援が投資であるということは大人でもわかるべき本質ではないでしょうか。

たとえば脱炭素を進めている企業や、地域社会の発展に貢献している企業の株式に投資するというのも We 視点の投資です。We の視点を投資だけでなく、消費にまで広げていくとしたら、たとえば環境に配慮した服を購入するとか、児童労働を経ていないチョコレートを買うといった「エシカル（ethical）消費」などが考えられます。

「そんなのは綺麗ごとで、最後はやはり自分の利益こそが大事」とおっしゃる方もいると思います。

でも、ここでよく考えてみてください。人間は一人で生きているわけではありません。必ずどこかのコミュニティに属しています。そのなかで Me の利益だけを主張するような人は、本当に豊かな、ウェルビーイングな人生を送っているといえるのでしょうか。

今回のコロナ禍で私たちは肌で感じたと思います。いかに Me、自分や家族の健康を守ることが重要であることが。しかし、Me だけに着眼を置いて、We が分断されてしまうと Me が何もできなくなる。We がきちんと回っているから Me の生活が成り立っているということに。

つまり Me から We へは決して Me の否定ではありません。Me から We へ、そして We から Me へという循環が重要であり、それが本章のテーマである「包摂性」にもつながっていくのです。

渋沢栄一は『論語と算盤』の「合理的経営」で、いまから100年以上前から警戒の鐘を鳴らしています。「**その経営者一人がいかに大富豪になっても、そのために社会の多数が貧困に陥るようなことでは、その幸福は継続されない**」

well-being.

Therefore, from "Me" to "We" is not a denial of "Me."

From "Me" to "We" and from "We" to "Me". This is the circle of life that leads us to the topic of chapter, inclusiveness.

Eiichi Shibusawa has been ringing the bell of vigilance for inclusiveness for more than 100 years ago. In "Rational Management" in *"Rongo and Sorban"* he says,

"No matter how much wealth the corporate executive accumulates, if most of society falls into poverty, then his well-being cannot continue."

Eiichi Shibusawa, the "Father of Japanese Capitalism", had an expectation from capitalism. It was not just enrichening the life of the few, but for society of well-being, where "no one is left behind." In order to achieve a society, a mind shift of using money from "Me" to "We" is in the calling.

日本資本主義の父である渋沢栄一が、近代的で豊かな社会をつくるために資本主義に期待していたことは、最近の論調のように一部の人たちが富を得るための仕組みではありませんでした。誰一人取り残されることない、多数のウェルビーイングが実現されている社会でありました。そのために必要なことは、Me から We へというお金の使い方のマインドシフトです。

誰一人取り残さない

　SDGs の基本中の基本の理念は「誰一人取り残さない」と表現されています。SDGs には「すべての人に健康と福祉を」「質の高い教育をみんなに」「安全な水とトイレを世界中に」「エネルギーをみんなに、そしてクリーンに」「平和と公正をすべての人に」というように、17のゴールが設定されていて、世界中の国がそのゴールの達成を目指して努力をしているわけですが、2030年という期限までに一部の国や地域がそれを達成できたとしても、実は成功とはいえません。

　壮大な青天を衝くような目標ですが、大事なことは、全世界の国々が達成することなのです。つまり「誰一人取り残さない」のが、SDGs にとって何よりも大事なことなのです。これが「包摂性＝インクルーシブ」の考え方です。

　では、SDGs 達成において銀行が考えるべき包摂性とは何なのでしょうか。

　それは、すべての人々が等しく金融サービスを受けられるようにすることです。

Leave No One Behind

The very essence of the SDGs is "leave no one behind." This means that the 17 goals must be achieved by 2030 for all countries, not just for the selected few. A very challenging goal for mankind indeed, but this is what "inclusiveness" means as defined by the SDGs.

So, in this context of the SDGs, what does "inclusiveness" mean for banks?

It is ensuring that all people have access to financial services.

According to the World Bank, the number of adults (over 15 years old) who do not have a bank account is 1.7 billion people, more than ten times the population of Japan. Moreover, this number is expected to increase as the global population increases.

Imagine living in a society where we can not have a bank account. You would have no choice but to hide the money

日本をはじめとする先進国で生活しているとなかなか実感できないのですが、世界銀行によると、銀行口座をもてない成人（世界銀行の定義によると15歳以上）は17億人に達するといわれています。日本の人口の10倍以上です。しかも世界的な人口の増加に伴って、その数はこれからも増え続けるのではないかとみられています。

　想像してみてください。銀行口座がもてなければどうなるのか。

　働いて得たお金を現金のまま、家のどこかに隠して保管するしかありません。当然のことですが、悪事を働く人はそれを知っていますから、強盗に入ろうとします。つまり治安が悪化し、人々は枕を高くして寝られなくなるでしょう。私たちが当たり前と思っている、ATMから現金を引き出すことも、あるいは通信販売などで買い物をしたときの決済などもいっさいできません。

　これは非常に不便です。だからこそ「ファイナンシャル・インクルージョン（金融包摂）」といって、貧困層も含めて世界中の地域社会において誰もが金融サービスを受けられる環境の構築が急がれているのです。

　そのための具体的な動きはすでにさまざまなところで行われています。たとえばバングラデシュのグラミン銀行のように、貧困層を対象にして少額資金を融資するマイクロファイナンスは、その一例です。

　では、地域金融機関にとっての金融包摂とは具体的に何を指すのでしょうか。

　日本国内に、銀行口座を開設できない人がいるということ自体が信じられないという人もいると思うのですが、現実にはいます。たとえば外国人労働者がそうです。

　海外の本社などから派遣されてくる外国人エリートに金融包摂の

that you earned, somewhere in your house. Of course, this would increase chances of robbery, and the security of living in your own house would be at risk.

That is why there is an urgent need for "financial inclusion" for all regional communities of this world.

For the underprivileged of the world, microfinance, like Grameen Bank in Bangladesh, is an example of financial inclusion.

So, what does financial inclusion mean specifically for the regional financial institutions?

It may be hard to believe that there are people in Japan who cannot open a bank account, but in reality, there are. For example, foreign workers.

The elite working for multi-national firms do not have problems regarding financial inclusion. Yet, many people from abroad, such as "foreign technical intern trainees" that work and live among us in Japanese society have difficulties in opening bank accounts.

For example, the Law on the Prevention of Transfer of Criminal Profits, amended in April, 2013 requires the person to confirm his/her occupation and the purpose of conducting transactions when opening an account. This has raised the hurdles to opening an account, especially for those whose Japanese is still not fluent.

There is also concern that when foreign workers leave Japan to return home, some of them may sell their bank ac-

問題はないでしょう。一方、外国人技能実習生をはじめとして、日本国内にも現場作業に従事している外国人労働者が大勢、日本人と共生しています。街を歩いていると、工事現場で働いている外国人労働者を見かけますし、コンビニエンスストアやファミリーレストランなどで働いている外国人も大勢います。

彼らの多くは日本の銀行に口座を開くことができません。

その理由はさまざまです。

たとえば、2013年4月に法改正された犯罪収益移転防止法（犯罪による収益の移転防止に関する法律）によって、口座を開設するにあたっては、本人の職業や取引を行う目的について確認が求められるようになり、特に日本語にまだ慣れていない外国人にとって、口座開設に至るまでのハードルが一段と引き上げられました。

あるいは、銀行預金を開設できた外国人労働者が帰国する際に、自分の口座を第三者に売却することもあるようで、それが主に犯罪組織などの不正送金やマネーロンダリングなどに利用されるケースが報告されています。

また、これは銀行側の事情ですが、外国への送金手続が煩雑であり、外国人労働者の海外送金がコストに見合わないため、外国人労働者の銀行口座開設に及び腰という面もあります。

そのため、海外に不正送金する地下銀行が暗躍する土壌が生まれてしまいます。犯罪を防ぐために設けられた制限が、さらなる不正の温床になる典型例です。ちなみに地下銀行とは、銀行法等に基づいた免許をもたず、海外送金などを不正に行っている業者のことです。

しかし、そもそも外国人労働者や技能実習生の全員が犯罪に手を染めているわけではもちろんありません。ほとんどが真面目に日本

count to third parties. There have been cases reported where these accounts have been used by criminal organizations for fraudulent remittances and money laundering.

In addition, some banks argue that because the procedure for overseas remittance of foreign workers is more complicated, it does not commensurate the cost. This also raises the bar for foreign workers to open bank accounts.

As a result, this situation brews an environment where uncertified, hence unregulated, so-called "underground banks" are created to transfers money overseas. It is ironic that restrictions to prevent crime is in fact providing a hotbed for possible injustices.

Of course, this does not mean all foreign workers and technical intern trainees are involved in crime. This is far from the truth. Most of them have come to Japan hoping for a bright future, diligently working and acquiring skills so that they can give their families a better life.

The regional communities in Japan can provide such a future for these foreign workers.

Crime prevention is essential. Yet if those people who are working diligently among us in society, are prevented from simply opening a bank account, that condition needs to be improved immediately. Without such inclusiveness, how can a regional community boast that they are truly prosperous.

It is a reality that foreign workers are essential to revitaliz-

で技能を身につけて、よりよい生活を自分たちの家族に与えたいという明るい未来を抱いて日本へ入国してきた人たちです。そのような未来を、彼らに提供する度量が日本の地域社会にあるはずです。

犯罪防止は不可欠ですが、そのための線引きを厳格に行うことで、日本で真面目に学んで、仕事をして、家族や社会に還元しようとしている人たちが銀行口座をもつことができない地域社会に、真の豊かさと繁栄が達成できるのでしょうか。

地域創生に、外国人労働者の存在が不可欠であるという現実があります。地域社会の繁栄に貢献している彼らに対してファイナンシャルインクルージョンや共生の解決策の対応に意識を寄せない状態で、SDGバッジを付けた胸を張ることはできません。

地元の若者のインクルージョン

ここでいう「地元の若者」とは、もともとそこで育った若者と、大都市圏から地方に移住した人の両方を含めて考えます。地域創生には「ワカモノ、ソトモノ、バカモノ」が必須と一般的にいわれていますから、豊かな地域社会において大切な存在である彼らの包摂性が不可欠であることに間違いないでしょう。

最近に始まったことではありませんが、若者を中心にして地方から大都市圏への人口移動が相変わらず続いています。

総務省が作成、公表している「住民基本台帳人口移動報告」によると、2019年の都道府県別転出入者数は、東京都、神奈川県、千葉県、埼玉県、愛知県、大阪府、福岡県、沖縄県は転入超ですが、それ以外の道府県は軒並み転出超でした。

ing the regional economies throughout Japan. If financial inclusion cannot be extended to those who are participating in the prosperity of the regional communities, the SDGs badge cannot be worn with honor.

Inclusion of the Local Youth

The term "local youth" applies to both who grew up within the community as well as those who moved in from other large metropolitan areas. It is said that "the young, the outsider, and the foolish (risk taker)" are necessary for the vitality of regional communities. Therefore, it is obvious and essential that "inclusiveness" of these important groups is of utmost importance.

According to the "Resident Register Population Migration Report" prepared and published by the Ministry of Internal Affairs and Communications, the number of people moving into Tokyo, Kanagawa, Chiba, Saitama, Aichi, Osaka, Fu-

正確な数字がないのですが、恐らく地方から大都市圏に移り住む人を年齢階層別に分けたら、若者が圧倒的に多いのではないでしょうか。その理由は、多くの人が察していると思いますが、若者にとって地域に魅力的な仕事が多くないからです。

　もちろん、その「魅力」とは経済的なことに限ったものではありません。自分がその地域にいることによる自己実現感が薄いと、東京や大阪などの大都市圏で生活したほうが刺激的だし、おもしろそうだと考える若者が増えるのは当然のことです。地方は高齢者層の存在感がまだまだ大きくて、この世代間ギャップによって、自分たちが育ったミュニティで自由に活躍できないと考えている若者層が一定数いるかもしれません。結果的に、若者層の地方からの人口流出を促している面があるのではないかと考えられます。

　一方、新型コロナウイルスの感染拡大を受けて、一部ではこれから地方におけるライフスタイルが脚光を浴びるのではないかと期待する声も出てきています。たしかに、一部の大手企業が本社を地方に移転させたり、リモートワークによって場所を選ばずに働けたりするなど、さまざまな動きが出てきました。「多拠点居住」のように定住場所を決めず、仕事の都合やその時の気分に応じて住む場所を変えていく、というライフスタイルも、徐々に認知されつつあります。

　つまり、仕事のためだけに都市圏に移住して地域から離れる必要がない時代の幕が上がりました。課題は、地域が若者たちに魅力ある生活を提供できるかにあります。地方が外部から来る人たちを受け入れる姿勢がなければ、大都市圏から地方へという人の流れも止まってしまい、動き出しつつあるせっかくの地方再認識のムードもなくなってしまうおそれがあります。

kuoka, and Okinawa in 2019 exceeded those moving out, while all other prefectures saw net outflow.

There are no accurate figures, but most of the outflow is likely to be the younger generation. The primary reason is probably because they feel that there are less attractive jobs in the regional communities.

Of course, "appeal" is not limited to economic opportunities, but many young people probably think that living in a metropolitan area such as Tokyo or Osaka is more exciting, especially if their sense of self-realization is subdued living in the community where they grew up. The generation gap present in the regional communities may be a part of the reason for the outflow of young people.

However, the Covid-19 crisis may change this flow, as the lifestyle in the regional communities have started to attract attention. Because "remote work" has become a norm and gives freedom to workers regarding location, some large companies have moved their headquarters and operations away from the big cities. The lifestyle of "multi-base residence" is becoming attractive to many.

This means that we have entered a new norm where there is no need to move to the large cities to find only work. The challenge is whether the regional community can provide attractive lifestyle to young people.

If the regional communities do not open their doors of inclusiveness to outsiders from the big cities, then the popula-

もともと住んでいた地元の若者だけでなく、地方での生活に魅力を感じて地方移住を考えている大都市圏居住の若者も含めてすべてを受け入れられるだけの包括性が地域になければ、これから先も地方は人口流出が続き、やがて財政危機に陥る自治体が増えていくおそれもあります。

　こうした時代の大きな潮流において、地域金融機関の役割への期待は高まります。

　大事なことは、MeからWeのメンタリティをもって地域の経済社会の土台をつくることだと思います。たとえば、地元の若者や外部から来る若者が新しい住居を構えることや新しい事業を立ち上げるに際して必要となる資金の出し手になる役割が求められているのでしょう。

　また、子連れの若い世代の居住の決め手は、子どもたちの教育環境だと思います。地元の教育委員会や学校に任せるだけではなく、地域の保育やアフタースクールを含めた教育環境をいかに整えるかに金融機関が貢献できる役割も多々あると思います。

　保育や教育に加え、美味しくて健康な食事や豊かな自然を子どもたちに提供できる環境は、リモートワークが可能で、したがって、比較的に高収入のある若者世代の多くに魅力的な地域になるのではないでしょうか。

　地元とともに、このような若手世代がインクルージョンを推進する事業は、もしかしたら今期の数字に直につながらないかもしれません。しかし、地域社会の持続可能な開発としてきわめて重要な目標です。

tion decline will just continue, to the demise of the fiscal base for the community.

With this population migration megatrend, the role of regional financial institutions will become more and more important. By promoting the mindset of "from Me to We," regional financial institutions should build the foundations for the regional economy, such as provide financing for housing for outsiders and launching of new businesses.

For young families with children, educational environment is a decisive factor. There are many roles that regional financial institutions can contribute towards creating an educational environment that, in addition to the public education system, includes childcare and after school in the community.

In addition to childcare and education, an environment that can provide children with delicious and healthy food, and the beauty of nature will be an attraction for many young people who can work remotely, and therefore likely to have a relatively higher income.

Projects such as these may not deliver to the bottom line in the current fiscal quarter. However, for the sustainable development of the regional community, it is a goal of utmost importance.

生活破綻者のインクルージョン

　生活破綻に追い込まれた人に、いかにして地域金融機関がかかわるかという問題についても考えたいと思います。

　ただ、すでに生活が破綻した人に対して金融機関が当面の生活費を融資するというのは、非現実的です。「銀行取引できない人を含むのはむずかしい」という金融機関の経営トップの正直な悩みも聞こえてきます。

　ただ繁栄する地域社会をパーパスとする担い手が、この問題に見て見ぬふりすることはできません。やはり大事なことはこれ以上、生活破綻者を出さないようにするための方策を考え、実行することであり、そのためにはやはり、「教育」と「雇用創出」の観点が必要です。

　渋沢栄一は『論語と算盤』の「防貧の第一要義」で、このような意見を述べています。

　「人に徒食悠遊させよというのではない。なるべく直接保護を避けて、防貧の方法を講じたい」

　これは、古代中国の思想家の老子の**「授人以魚　不如授人以漁**──飢えている人に魚をとってあげれば、一日は食べられるけれど、魚のとり方を教えれば、彼は一生食べることができる」という格言に類似している考え方であります。

　たとえば、金融機関における文脈での教育というのは、「金銭教育」があります。中学校・高等学校などで投資教育を行っているという話が時々、ニュースになりますが、ここでいう金銭教育は、投資教育以前の問題です。

Inclusion of the Financially Distressed

For regional financial institutions, "inclusiveness" of the financially distressed poses challenges since it is unrealistic to provide financing to those that are bankrupt.

However, it is a problem that, as the caretaker of a prosperous regional community, regional financial institutions cannot turn a blind eye. It is imperative to prevent further financial distress in the community, and in that respect "education" and "job creation" are important.

Eiichi Shibusawa expresses his perspectives in "The First Key to Poverty Prevention" of *"Rongo and Soroban."*

"Providing the people food and comforts freely is not the answer. We should avoid providing direct welfare protection as much as possible, but rather take measures to prevent poverty."

This is similar thinking to the ancient Chinese philosopher Lao Zi's teachings, **"If you catch a fish and give to him, he can eat it for a day, but if you teach him how to fish, he can eat for the rest of his life."**

In this context, a role that regional financial institutions can play is "financial education." However, this education is not limited to formal education in middle and high schools, but also in real life situations.

"Consume according to your income."

「自分の身の丈にあった消費をする」

「クレジットカードで浪費をしない」

「健全な消費を心がける」

「節約のしすぎは健康を害し、むしろ余計な支出を増やすおそれがある」

「金融機関との付き合い方」

「怪しい利殖話の見極め方」

など、考えるべきことはいろいろあります。

　この手の知識を子どもたちに身につけさせる勉強を、日本の学校では長いこと疎かにしてきました。お金のことを考えることは卑しいという固定概念があったのでしょうか。だからこそ、コモンズこどもトラストセミナーの「4つのお金の使い方」は大事な活動だと思っています。

　このような知識を子どものうちから身につけたのと、まったく知らずに大人になるのとでは、お金との付き合い方が大きく変わってきます。

　一人でも生活破綻者を減らすために、この手の金銭教育を、一人でも多くの子どもたちに伝えていく努力をするべきでしょう。それを地域金融機関だけで行うのがむずかしいのであれば、ファイナンシャル・プランナーのような外部の専門家と連携するという選択肢もあります。

　また、「教育」と同様に、生活破綻者に陥ることを防止するために重要なのが「雇用創出」です。いくら金銭教育が施されたとしても、そもそもお金を稼ぐ方法がなかったら、生活そのものができなくなります。日本の「ファイナンシャル・リテラシー」、金融教育は、お金の源になる「働き」から生じる「価値」への意識が疎かで

"Do not overspend with credit cards."

"Consume with prudence."

"Excessive cost-cutting can harm your physical health and as a result may increase extra spending."

"How to get along with financial institutions."

"How to identify suspicious ponzi schemes"

The Japanese society has generally considered it a taboo to teach children about money, and thus financial literacy has been neglected in the education system. That is exactly the reason why offering "Commons Kodomo (Child) Trust Seminar" and having children think about money is such an important activity.

Having the knowledge about the basic fundamentals of money as a child will have impact on how you handle money as an adult. Even the possibility of one person from falling into financial distress makes it worth the effort.

If internal resources are limited for such activities, there are always external financial planners who are willing to co-operate.

"Job creation" is also another important factor in preventing financial distress in the community.

Education about money is useless, unless there are means to earn money in the community. In fact, the problem with the educational contents for "financial literacy" in Japan is that it often does not take into account value creation arising from work, which is the source of money in the first place.

はないかと感じています。

　短期的な解決策ではありません。ただ、だからこそ、地元の若い人たちや、大都市圏からの移住を希望している若い人たちが地元で起業するのを、地域金融機関がサポートする意味があるのです。生活破綻者を含む社会の弱者のインクルージョンを役所任せにするだけではなく、地域金融機関が工夫することに意味があるのです。

　このような社会的課題への意識を高めている地域金融機関が年々増えていることは良い傾向です。いままでの時代の常識で束縛することなく、新たなチャレンジを後押しする金融が、地域社会の未来の実現にきわめて重要です。

It is not a short-term solution. Yet, providing finance and support for creation of new businesses in the community is a very important role for regional financial institutions. Providing "inclusiveness" for the financially distressed and other underprivileged members of society is not just the responsibility for the local government. There are plenty of rooms for new innovation from regional financial institutions.

It is a very good trend that year by year, the number of regional financial institutions that are becoming more aware of their role in this kind of "inclusiveness" are increasing. Financing that are not tied to norms of the past, but supports new challenges in this current world environment is essential in realizing the future of the regional community.

第3章

参　画　性
─全員参加型で取り組む─

Chapter 3　●　Participatory Approach
── Everyone Participates ──

包摂性と参画性の違いについて

　前章で説明した包摂性は、「誰一人取り残さない」という意味があり、SDGs の理念そのものでした。

　これに対して参画性は、「全員参加型で取り組む」ことを意味しています。

　「誰一人取り残さない」と「全員参加型で取り組む」。

　字面を眺めると、両者とも同じような意味合いをもっているように感じるのではないでしょうか。

　とはいえ、このように異なる言葉で並列してあげられているのですから、その意味は当然ですが違います。

　では、何が違うのでしょうか。

　前述した包摂性は、「誰一人取り残さない（社会を創る）」というように、「社会」という大きな枠組みのなかで誰一人取り残さないという意味合いがあります。つまり、金融機関として、地域社会において「誰一人取り残さない」ために務めるということです。

　一方、参画性は特定のコミュニティに属する人は全員参加で事にあたるという意味をもっています。これを地域金融機関に当てはめると、そこに所属する人が皆、与えられた仕事を自分コトとしてとらえ、皆で力をあわせ、全員参加型で取り組んでいくというイメージを思い描いていただければよいと思います。

　わかりやすくいえば、社外に目を向けているのが包摂性であり、社内に目を向けているのが参画性です。地域金融機関の参画性への課題は具体的に、若手層と女性です。

　ただ、地域金融機関の参画性に焦点を当てたとき、かなり危機的

Difference Between Inclusiveness and Participatory Approach ～～～～

As discussed in the previous chapter, "inclusiveness" is to "leave no one behind." In this chapter, we will explore "participatory approach" which means "everyone participates."

Sounds like similar concepts. So, what is the difference?

Inclusiveness is about the larger framework of society, so in the case for regional financial institution, it is to "leave no one behind" in the local community.

On the other hand, "participatory approach" is about the organization itself, rather than the community at large. Another way to look at it, "inclusiveness" is the "why" question, whereas the "participatory approach" is the "how" question.

To put it simply, inclusiveness is talking about people outside the company, and participatory approach is talking about people inside the company. For regional financial institutions, the challenges of the participatory approach are specifically, younger generation and women.

From the top management of regional financial institutions, the following concerns were raised.

"It is a big problem that young people are quitting."

"They thought they joined the top company in their regional community, but became disillusioned with the reality."

な状況に直面しているのではないかと懸念しています。

　というのも、次のような声が経営トップから聞こえてくるのです。

「若年層が辞めていくのは大問題」

「地域一番の企業のはずなのに失望して辞める」

「自己実現なされないからと、早期に辞める」

「どの会社でも熱い想いを原点にもっている人がいる。けれども、活かせていない」

　特に30歳前後の若手行員、女性行員に辞める人が多いようです。

　いまの30代行員は、10年後、20年後に組織の幹部となって地域金融機関を支えていく存在です。その若手たちが組織に背中を向け始めているのです。これは、地域金融機関の組織になんらかの問題が生じているとしか考えられません。

　いや、この手の傾向は地域金融機関に限った話ではないと思います。対面型証券会社のなかにも、若手営業社員が次々に辞めているという話をよく耳にします。

　なぜ、対面型証券会社の若手営業担当者が、次々に辞表を提出して辞めているのでしょうか。

　一番の理由は、自分たちが日々行っている仕事が、本当に社会のためになっているのかということに対する疑問です。証券会社といえば、いまでもかなり厳しいノルマが課せられています。「ノルマ」という言葉が「営業目標」という言葉などに入れ替わっていますが、日々の株式の売買手数料に加えて国内外の債券、投資信託、保険など、さまざまな金融商品に数値目標が設定されています。それを何としてでも達成しなければならない状況のなかで、「自分たちがお客様に勧めている金融商品を購入することで、本当にお客様は

"They quit early because they do not feel a sense of self-fulfillment working at the bank."

"Every company has people that are passionate at their core, yet it is not being utilized by the bank."

In particular, young bankers around 30 years old and women in general have shown tendency to leave the bank for other career paths.

Bankers in their 30s are the generation that will be supporting the organization in managerial positions in 10 or 20 years. If these young people are starting to turn their backs on the organization, this can only spell trouble for the future of regional financial institutions.

Yet, this trend is not limited to regional financial institutions. Same kind of stories can be heard at securities brokers as well.

Instead of pushing products that they do not think offers much benefit to the customers, some of them are setting up their independent companies as IFAs (independent financial advisors), in order to offer products that they feel confident in delivering.

This is a big headache for the brokerage firms, since it tends to be the best and brightest that tends to leave the nest to start their own businesses. This is also the same for the banks as well.

Many people complain about the attitudes of "young people these days." However, a president of a regional financial

幸せになれているのだろうか」と考え始めたのです。

　その結果、自分たちに課せられたノルマを消化するために、お客様にとって不利な金融商品を販売していることに嫌気を感じた若手営業担当者が勤め先の証券会社を辞めて、IFA（独立系ファイナンシャル・アドバイザー）など新しい金融サービスを立ち上げる動きが、目立つようになってきました。こうして大証券会社からスピンアウトした若手が口をそろえていうのは、「前の会社では顧客本位の営業ができなかった。それを新しいビジネスで実現したい」ということなのです。

　会社にとって頭が痛いことは、落ちこぼれが辞めていくということでなく、有望な若手たちこそが、自分たちのパーパスに忠実に働きたいと飛び出してしまうことです。

　恐らく、地域金融機関でも同じような傾向が起きているのではないでしょうか。10年後、20年後に地域金融機関を背負うべき若手行員が次々に辞めていくような銀行では未来を拓くことができない。だからこそ参画性がこれまで以上に求められているのです。

　「最近の若者は」という口癖は、どの時代でもあったと思います。しかし、「中間層の50代の管理職が自分たちの成功体験を20代、30代に伝えきれてない」という現状が、お話をお伺いした地域金融機関の経営トップのお話から見えています。

　渋沢栄一の時代も同じような現象があったと思います。ただ、そのなかで、栄一は指摘しています。

　「昔の少数の偉い青年と現代の一般青年と比較してかれこれ言うことは少し間違っている。今の青年の中にも偉い者もあれば、昔の青年にも偉くない者もあった」

　有望な若者は、どの時代でも存在しているのです。これからの高

institution conveyed to me that he is concerned about the middle managers in their 50s that are unable to convey their experiences of success properly to their colleagues in the 20s and 30s, in the context of the present environment.

There were probably similar complaints about the "young people these days" in Eiichi Shibusawa's days as well. But he observed the following.

"It is a bit wrong to compare the few great young men of the days past with the ordinary young men of today. There are also great young people in the present days and there were also plenty of those who were not great men in the days past."

Promising young people exist during any age. However, in Japan, where the aging population and declining birthrate are accelerating, retention of talented young people in their organizations are critical.

These "walls" within the organization that prevent promising young people from expressing their purpose should be torn down immediately.

The SDGs can be utilized as a means where organizations can invigorate capabilities and initiatives of the young and at the same time open eyes of those in middle management.

Start a project team consisting of young bankers in their 20s and 30s and call for proposal new businesses that will lead to achieving the SDGs. Give the best team a real budget allocation.

齢化・少子化が加速する日本社会で、有望な若者にいかに入社してもらい、彼らの可能性を発揮してもらうかは、すべての企業が直面する大きな課題です。

　有望な若手が切磋琢磨して活躍をすることに組織内で壁が立ちはだかっているとしたら、それを取り除いて参画性のポテンシャルを活かすことが、時代の節目に立っている現在であるからこそきわめて重要です。

　若手行員の参画性に危機感を覚えている地域金融機関の経営トップへご提案があります。SDGs を活用して、若手行員の参画意識を高め、かつ、中間管理職にも刺激を与える策です。

　20代、30代の若手プロジェクト・チームを立ち上げて、SDGs の達成を導く社会的課題解決の新規事業の提案を募り、そして、最優秀チームに実弾の予算配分を与えてください。失敗したら、組織として「ちょっと痛い」と思うぐらいの規模であることが重要だと思います。そして、そのチームには組織内外のすべてのリソースやネットワークを自由に駆使し、その成果を直接、経営トップへ報告することもカギです。

　失敗を恐れる若手が手をあげられるような取組みではありません。しかし、どの地域金融機関でも、必ず手をあげてくる若手がいるに違いありません。そして、ほぉ～と感心する、アッと驚くような事業案を発掘してくるでしょう。

　渋沢栄一はいいました。

　「新しき時代には新しき人物を養成して新しき事物を処理せぬばならない」（『渋沢栄一 訓言集』学問と教育）と。

　参画性なき組織に、このような新規時代に相応しい人材が集まるわけがなく、残るわけがありません。

The size of the budget is important. It should be large enough, so that if it doesn't work out, the bank will feel a bit of pain.

Give the project team access to all resources within and outside the organization. The most important aspect is to have the project team report directly to top management.

Some will probably shrink away because of the fear of failure. However, there must be a group young people in every regional institution who will eagerly raise their hands for such an opportunity. And, most likely, they will surprise all with a new business model.

Eiichi Shibusawa said.

"In the new era, we must cultivate new people who can create new endeavors."

There is no way that such "new people" as Eiichi defintes, will join and remain in an organization without the participatory approach.

女性の活用や登用ではなく、活躍 〜

　日本のバブル経済が崩壊した1990年代は、株価や地価が底なし沼にはまり込んだように下がり続け、景気が一気に悪くなり、企業業績がどんどん落ち込み、金融機関は多額の不良債権を抱え込んでにっちもさっちもいかなくなった時代でした。知り合いの外国人はシレっとした顔をして「日本なんて何も心配することないよ。大丈夫」といいました。その理由を聞いてみると、「だってこれまでの日本の成功って、人口の半分も使っていないじゃない」ということでした。

　「なるほど」と思ったことを覚えています。日本経済は戦後の廃墟から見事に立ち直り、1980年代にはバブル経済が醸成されるほど発展しましたが、たしかに当時、企業は男性社会であり、女性は男性のアシスタント的な仕事しか与えられていませんでした。そして25歳くらいまでに結婚して会社を辞めるというのが普通だったのです。

　当時は、女性が25歳を過ぎると「クリスマス・ケーキ」になる、つまり、クリスマスが過ぎると誰も見向きをしないという、いまではNGな表現が女性自身からも発されていました。

　そう考えると当時の日本は、総人口の半分も働いていない状態で、あれだけの経済復興・発展を実現させたのですから、知り合いの外国人がいったように、完全に死んだわけではなかったのです。

　そして、渋沢栄一はいまから100年ぐらい前、『論語と算盤』の「偉人とその母」で、このような考えを示しています。

「果たしてしからば女子に対する旧来の侮蔑的観念を除却し、女

Not Utilization or Promotion, but Rather the Action 〜〜〜〜〜〜〜

In the 1990s, Japan's bubble economy collapsed. Stock prices and land prices fell of a cliff and became stuck in a bottomless swamp. The economy became limp, corporate performance fell, and financial institutions were paralyzed with large amounts of bad debt.

However, an acquaintance of mine from overseas made an observation. "I wouldn't worry too much about Japan," he says, "You guys achieve all this with only half the population!"

How true. The Japanese economy recovered brilliantly from the ruins of the post-war period, and by the 1980s it developed to the extent that a bubble economy was created. And, male-dominated companies were the norm and women's role was being the assistant.

Those days, it was normal for a woman to get married by the age 25 years old and quit the company. Back then, the women even referred to themselves as a "Christmas Cake," leftovers that nobody would want to touch after the 25th, a description that would be a very politically incorrect these days.

Therefore, it was a fairly accurate description to say that the post-war "Japanese miracle" was achieved with half of the total population.

子も男子同様国民としての才能智徳を与え、共に相助けて事を為さしめたならば、従来五千万の国民中二千五百万人しか用をなさなかった者が、さらに二千五百万人を活用せしめる事となるではないか」

　ある意味、安倍前首相が掲げた「１億総活躍社会」のようなものですが、いまの日本はまだまだ優秀な人材が埋もれていて活躍していないケースが目立ちます。

　国連が示したSDGsの５つPのPeople、人間の基本的ニーズであるゴール５：「ジェンダー平等を実現しよう」という意味で、日本はいまだに100～150年前の新興国・発展途上国と変わっていないといいたくありません。しかし、現実として、さまざまなジェンダー・ダイバーシティの世界ランキングでは、先進国のみならず、新興国・発展途上国を含んでも最下位というケースが少なくない残念な現状です。

　何のひいき目ももたずに見ると、それぞれの地域社会において、地域金融機関に働いている女性は、非常に優秀です。その優秀な人材を活かし切れていないとしたら、それは経営の怠慢以外の何物でもありません。

　現に、地域金融機関の経営トップから、現状が聞こえてきます。
「銀行の半分が女性であるが、幹部にはなっていない」
「支店長で女性はゼロ。出したいと思っているが」
「女性は係長・支店長まで。いままでロールモデルがなかった」
　しかしながら、女性が組織に参画するというと、世の男性はこう思うかもしれません。「男でも辛い仕事なのに女性が耐えられるわけがない」。
　でも、そうでしょうか。私が企業経営者との問題意識で立ち上げ

About 100 years ago, Eiichi Shibusawa expressed the exact same observation.

"If we remove the old contemptuous notion of women, give women the talent and wisdom as well as given to the men, then wouldn't it be possible for the other half of the 50 million to actively participate in society?"

100 to 150 years ago, when Eiichi made this statement, Japan was an emerging country. Yet, in the present day, it is regrettable to see that in the ranking for women empowerment, Japan is at the bottom of the list, not only developed countries but also emerging and developing countries as well.

Women who work at regional financial institutions are extremely bright and talented. If this talent is not empowered, bringing value to the organization and community, then it can be stated straightforward that the management should be blamed for neglect.

The concerns regarding diversity echoes among top management of regional financial institutions.

"Half of the bank are women, but no executives."

"We have no women branch managers. We need some."

"Women have made it to division chief or branch manager, but no role mode until recent years."

When the topic of gender diversity is brought up, the usual push-back is that "Women can't bear men's hard job."

Really? Is this true? In a program that supports Japanese

た「アフリカ起業支援コンソーシアム」（http://entre-africa.jp）でアフリカという過酷な事業環境で起業にチャレンジする若手日本人を支援していましたが、その大半が女性でした。途中で音を上げて退場して帰国する起業家もいましたが、それは男性たちでした。

「辛い仕事」と「つまらない仕事」は違います。

そもそも男女でも同じ仕事を同じようにこなすべきだという考えは、ダイバーシティの本質がわかっていません。いろいろな価値観を同質化させることではなく、同じところでさまざまな価値観を取り入れる適材適所で新たな価値を生みだすことが参画性というダイバーシティです。

たとえばおもしろい支店づくりをしている地域金融機関もあります。通常、対面型の取引を行っている金融機関は、カウンターを挟んで銀行員とお客様が対峙しています。ただ、ここではカウンターを撤去してソファやテーブル席を設け、来店したお客様がくつろげる空間がつくられています。しかもその一角には、子どもが大きな丸いソファの上でゴロゴロしても大丈夫なスペースまで設けられています。

こうした店づくりは男性行員やベテランではまず思いつかないでしょう。このように女性目線を大切にした店づくりは、特にこれからの金融機関のリアル店舗では大切になってくると思います。

この金融機関の経営トップは「銀行のなかのカウンターから外を見るクセがある」ことに問題意識をもたれ、実験的にこのような店舗を立ち上げました。

また、別の経営トップからは「次の次のトップが女性であっても不思議ではない」という未来像を教えていただきました。

ジェンダー・ダイバーシティにおいて、言葉の細かい使い方では

entrepreneurs in Africa (http://entre-africa.jp) that I established with corporate executives who shared the same vision, we were surprised to see the most of the applicants and awardees were women. And, of the few awardees that gave up and came back to Japan, all of them were men.

It is absurd to think that men and women should do the same work in the same way. That is not the essence of diversity. Diversity is not about homogenizing various values, but rather incorporating different values to achieve the same goal.

An interesting model for diversity in real practice is provided by an innovative branch at a regional financial institution. There are no bank counters there, and it looks more like a neighborhood café. There is a large round sofa where small kids and babies can roll around.

A male branch member probably would have not come up with such an idea. All people working at this branch are women, including the branch manager.

The top management of this financial institution was aware of the problem that "there is a bad habit of bankers looking out towards the outside world from behind the counter of the bank."

Top management of another regional financial institution told me that he would not be surprised if his successor's successor was a woman.

In terms gender diversity, I believe it is important not use

ありますが、次のことに結構大事な要素が含まれていると思います。人数が足りないから働いてくれという女性の「活用」ではなく、幹部に女性を「登用」することでもなく、あくまでも女性の「活躍」が本質です。

とある経営トップに示していただいたように「なるほど、そういう発想があったのか」という女性の価値観、「存在力」や「意欲」をもっての活躍が重要なポイントです。女性が男性のようになることにダイバーシティを活かす参画性の本質があるとは思えません。

地域金融機関も新しいビジネスを真剣に考えなければならない時期にきているのです。だからこそ女性も若手も分け隔てなく活躍できる場を提供し、適材適所で皆が力を発揮できる場を築いていく必要があるのです。

間違いや失敗を責めない

適材適所で皆が力を発揮して、日常の仕事に参画しようという気持ちを皆にもってもらうためには、経営陣が現場の声に耳を傾ける必要があります。

これまで多くの金融機関は、本部からのトップダウンで営業方針、選定商品・サービスが現場の支店に指示されるという流れが一般的でした。ただ、本部スタッフは現場にかかわっていないので、どこまで現場の声、ひいてはお客様の声を把握しているのかという

the word "utilization" of women, to work because Japan is running out of people to work. Also, it is not the "promotion" of women to executives. But rather it is the "actions" by women.

As one top management pointed out, "I wouldn't have come up with an idea like that." The important point regarding empowerment of women is to deliver values and perspectives that men often lack. Diversity is not about expecting women to think and act like men in the working environment.

The present is a critical point of time where regional financial institutions must seriously consider new business opportunities. That is why it is essential to provide a working environment where both women and young people are empowered to play an active part.

Don't Blame Mistakes or Failures

The management needs to listen to the voices that rises from the front-line of their business so that everyone can work in their particular roles that matches their particular skills.

For many financial institutions, the standard mode of operation is for the corporate headquarters to instructed branch offices in a top-down approach regarding sales policies,

と、いささか疑問に思わざるをえません。

　大事なのは現場で実際にお客様の応対にあたっている女性行員、若手行員の声なのです。

　私がお話をお伺いした地域金融機関のなかで、営業目標の設定をやめたというところがいくつかあります。

　従来は本部が数字を決めて、それを各支店に割り振った後、支店側はそれを営業担当者の役職、年次などに応じて各人に割り振っていきます。こうして各人の営業目標が設定された後は、その目標を達成するために我武者羅になって、営業担当者全員が１カ月間、ひた走りに走るというものでした。それをやめてしまったのです。

　もちろん、そうはいっても何の目標もなければ、誰も働かなくなってしまいますから、目標設定は必要です。ただ、その目標設定の流れが、本部から現場に下りてくるのではなく、現場からの積上げ方式になっているのです。

　ただし、現場からあがってくる目標値に対して本部が何もいわないと、今度は現場が甘い目標設定を出してくるおそれがあるので、実際にそういう数字があがってきたときは、本部とディスカッションをしながら最適値を再設定します。

　やはり最初は業績が落ち込んだそうです。いままで上からの命令でやらされていたのが、いざ自分たちで決めるということになると、最適値をどこに設定すればよいのか迷いが生じます。また、本部からの営業目標に対するプレッシャーがなくなる分、現場のモチベーションが後退したことも、以前に比べて業績が落ち込んだ理由の一つだと思われます。

　ところが、さらに時間が経過すると、「この銀行は自分たちが支えているんだ」という現場のプライドが持ち上がってきて、「この

product selection and services. However, because headquarter staff does not work on the front-line of the branches, they often cannot hear the voice directly from the bank's customers.

Therefore, it is important for headquarters to pay attention to the observations and opinions of women and younger staff who are on the front line, dealing with customers on a daily basis.

Some of the regional financial institutions I interviewed have discontinued setting sales targets for their branches. In the past it was headquarters that set sales targets, and branches had to scramble to achieve their monthly quotas. But, they stopped all that.

Of course, if there is no goal setting, motivations tend to suffer. However, goal setting from bottom-up from the branches to headquarters is an innovation in operations flow that some regional financial institutions have decided to undertake.

However, if the headquarters has no say about the target, then there will be risk that they will be more laxed. So, there are discussions between headquarters and the branches regarding proposal in order to come up with the most suitable targets.

Even with this process, business performance fell initially.

However, as time passed, the pride of the bankers at the front-line began to rise, and the mood improved. Remarks

ままでは駄目だ」というムードが徐々に高まってきたそうです。自分コトに腹落ちできたのです。

その結果、「こうすればよいのではないか」「ああすれば数字につながるのではないか」というアイデアが、現場から次々にあがってくるようになったそうです。

これこそがまさに参画性です。行内で、これまでは主戦力としてみなされてこなかった女性行員や若手行員も、支店の数字が悪化すればそれを何とかしようという意識から、自ら積極的に対応策を考えて提案するようになったというのです。

製造業の現場では「QCサークル運動」というのがあります。これは同じ職場内で、品質管理活動を自発的に行う集まりのことで、この活動を通じて製品のクオリティが維持されています。自動車メーカーにしても、家電メーカーにしても、この手の努力を連綿と続けてきたことが、いまの高品質製品につながっているのです。

しかし、一方で金融セクターには、一般に、この手の努力が足りなかったように思えます。本部が決めたこと、あるいは金融行政が決めたことをただひたすら守っていれば商売を続けることができるという特異体質があったためでしょう。お上のいうとおりにしていれば何とか生き残れてきたのです。

これでは自分の頭で考えて実行に移すという力がなくなるのも当然です。

しかも日本の金融業界はかなり厳しい規制に長年守られてきましたから、なおのことです。

ちょっと厳しい言い方になってしまいますが、銀行という組織全体が指示待ちになっていたのだとしたら、そこに所属している行員が指示待ちになるのは、当然の成り行きですし、参画性が育たない

such as "it is us who are supporting this bank" started being heard. There was a good flow of new ideas that were initiated from the front-line.

This indeed is the participatory approach. Women and young staff members who thought they were not regarded as the main force in the bank, started to speak up and take initiative.

In the manufacturing sector, "QC" (Quality Circle) is a usual mode of operation. The voluntary gathering and adopting quality control activities within the workplace, improved the quality of products dramatically by this kind of kind of informal activities. This kind of continuous efforts by automakers and other manufacturers have led to today's Japan's high-quality products.

On the other hand, it appears the financial sector seems to have lagged behind this kind of efforts. The reason is probably because the norm was that decisions were made at headquarters or the government regulators and the front-line branches simply followed the rules.

All you need to do was followed the rules, and you were fine.

It is only natural that in this kind of environment, the power to think for yourself wanes. Moreover, Japan's financial industry has been in effect protected by quite strict regulations for many years, exacerbating this condition.

If the entire bank organization was simply waiting for in-

のも無理はありません。

　では、どうすれば参画性が育つのでしょうか。その答えを見つけるためには、逆になぜ指示待ちなのかを考えるとよいのかもしれません。

　指示待ちなのは、「指示された以外のことをやってはいけない」というメンタリティが強く働いているからでしょう。自分の独断で指示された以外のことをやって失敗したら怒られるのではないか。怒られるだけでなく減給されるのではないか。あるいは出世の道が閉ざされるのではないか、という気持ちがあって、自分から何かを提案して動くという傾向が鈍化することです。

　この指示待ち体質は、恐らく規制業種である金融機関だからこそ非常に強く出ているところはあるのだけれども、他の日本の組織にも多かれ少なかれあることだと思っています。

　銀行を日本で初めてつくった渋沢栄一が、現在の状況を見たら、何をいうでしょう。

　100年ぐらい前に、栄一は、このようにいっていました。

　「事業の方では、軍事上の事務のように一々上官の命令を待っているようでは、とかく好機を逃し易いので何事も命令を受けてやるという具合では一寸発達ということはむずかしいのである」

　いまでも、同じような奨励で喝を入れるのではないでしょうか。

　たとえば日本のモノづくり精神の開発には、「ベータ版」の発想はありません。日本の金融業界でも間違うことは致命的です。でも、米国のソフトウエア開発では、まずベータ版を出して使ってもらい、利用者から「ここがおかしい」などといった意見を集めて修正し、徐々に完成品に近づけていくというプロセスをたどります。

　これは、他のどこの会社よりも早く市場に投入することで競争に

structions to come down from top, it would be only natural for bank employees' sense of participatory approach cannot be cultivated.

Waiting for instructions was probably engraved in the minds of bankers probably because if they do something on their own initiative but end up failing, that may cost them the path of promotion. And that kind of fear keeps many from taking the initiative.

This mentality must change. It is probably more prevalent in the financial industry because it is a regulated industry, but all industry in Japan shares this to some extent or another.

What would Eiichi Shibusawa, who created the first bank in Japan, would day about this condition. Well, he said this about a 100 years ago:

"In business, if you are just waiting for orders from your superiors like the military, you will miss opportunities."

I think Eiichi would exclaim the exact message, if he were here today.

For example, in Japanese manufacturing there is no concept of the "beta" version like in American software industries. Let the customer use the beta version and if there is a bug then we will fix it, is a concept that Japanese financial industry just cannot imagine because a mistake is seen as fatal.

In the software industry, because the competition is so se-

勝つという考え方があるからですが、それができるのは間違いや失敗をタブー視していないからでもあります。だから、米国ではさまざまなスタートアップ企業が誕生するのです。

スタートアップ企業は、「この商品、サービスで世の中をもっと便利にしたい」という気持ちがあるからこそ、スタートアップ企業たりえるわけですが、それは社会への参画性の発露であるともいえます。

つまり日本の地域金融機関内に参画性を育むためには、間違いや失敗を恐れない、間違いや失敗をした人を責めない体質を築き上げることに尽きるのではないかと思うのです。

渋沢栄一は『論語と算盤』で「細心にして大胆になれ」と激励しています。

「従来の事業を大事に保守し、あるいは過失失敗をおそれてためらう弱い気力では到底国運のあとへひく」

これは、国運のみならず、地域運、社運も同じです。

また、同じく『論語と算盤』の「成敗は身に残る糟粕」では、このような指摘もしています。

「一時の成敗は長い人生、価値の多い生涯における泡沫のごときものである。しかるにこの泡沫のごときものに憧れて目前の成敗のみを論ずる者が多いようでは国家の発達進歩も思いやられる」

たしかにそうです。もし、SDGsを本気で取り込んでも、どうせ達成できない、失敗はしたくないという懸念で躊躇しているとしたら、栄一は「目前ではなく、青天を衝け！」と檄を飛ばすことに間違いありません。SDGsも長い生涯において通過点にすぎません。その次の、そしてさらにその次のゴールに手を伸ばすことで発達進歩が期待できるのです。

vere, speed is of the essence. In this context, a mistake is not a taboo, as long as it can be fixed.

In other words, in order to cultivate the participatory approach within Japan's regional financial institutions, it is of utmost necessity to build a code of principles that does not fear mistakes or failures, and do not blame those who made mistakes or failures.

Eiichi Shibusawa said the following.

"Just conserving the present state of business or the fear of failure will inevitably lead to decline of the state of the nation."

This not only applies to the state of nation, but also the regional community, and the company.

Similarly, Eiichi observes the following,

"Success or failure at some point in time is merely a bubble in one's long life. If there are many who find great value in this bubble, then the future development of our nation is in jeopardy."

A very good point. If there are hesitancies about the SDGs because there are concerns about not being able to achieve and fail, with no doubt, Eiichi will shout out, "Keep heads high! Blue skies above!"

The SDGs are just a passing point in a long lifetime. For certain, there will be another goal setting after SDGs. And after that. And after that. We can only expect progress, by reaching out.

第4章

統　合　性
—地域のウェルビーイングの総合プロデュース—

Chapter 4　●　Integrated Approach
— Producer of Regional Well-Being —

地域金融機関から地域振興機関へ ～～

　ある地域金融機関の経営トップが、本書のオンライン取材でおもしろいことをご指摘されました。

　「地域金融機関という言葉はある意味、昔の考え方であって、これからは地域振興機関になるべきだ」

　地域金融機関というと、行員がスクーターに乗って地元の家を一軒一軒回って預金を集め、そのお金を地元の中堅中小企業に貸すことで金利差を得るというイメージが強いのですが、もはやいまの時代にそれをメインにしている地域金融機関など、ほぼ皆無といってもよいでしょう。

　高度経済成長期のように、経済のパイがどんどん拡大していくなかで、企業の資金需要がきわめて強い状況下ならそれでも十分ビジネスは成り立ちますが、昨今のように経済が成熟期に入り、規模の拡大はほぼ望めず、しかも超低金利、マイナス金利が常態化している状況下では、この手の預貸ビジネスに依存している金融機関は早晩、経営が行き詰まります。

　その厳しい現実が多くの地域金融機関の経営者はわかっていますから、別の収益源として投資信託や保険の販売に力点を置いた経営方針を打ち出しているのです。

　ただ、それもある意味、限界に近いところに来ているような気がします。前述したように、地元に貢献したい、地元の人々のために働きたいと考えて地域金融機関に入った若い人たちが、自分たちの給料を得るために、本当の意味で地元の人々の役に立っているかどうかわからないような金融商品を販売しなければならないことに対

From Regional Financial Institutions to Regional Development Institutions ◂◂

During the interview for this book, president of a regional financial institution shared his perspective that "The word "regional financial institutions" is from the past. We should be called "regional development institutions" from now on."

The traditional image of "regional financial institutions" were bank employees riding their scooters though the community collecting deposits from households, lending the money to local small and medium-sized enterprises, and earning the interest rate spread. The more deposits they collected, the more money they made. However, in reality, those days are gone.

With the maturing economy, it is almost impossible to scale their banking business. And the ultra-low interest rates have become the norm, and financial institutions that rely only on deposit and loan business is facing a dead end street. Many have been turning to selling mutual funds and insurance as other sources of income.

But even this kind of fee-business is starting to reach the limit. As discussed in the previous chapter, many young people eager to contribute to their communities have begun to question their work. The future generation are losing their ambitions as bankers and are starting to write resignation letters.

して、疑問を抱き始めたのです。

　投資信託や保険商品を販売して手数料を稼ぐというビジネスモデルは、預貸によって金利差を得るという伝統的な銀行ビジネスが機能不全に陥ったなかで、落ち込んだ収益を補完するものとなりましたが、今度はそれを積極的に展開すればするほど、地域金融機関の若手を苦しめ、志半ばで辞表を書かざるをえないところまで追い込んでしまったのです。

　もちろん、そうはいっても地域金融機関は一民間企業ですから、なんらかのかたちで収益を生み出さなければなりません。それは一体、何なのでしょうか。そこであらためて考えたいのは、企業とは一体、何のために存在しているのか、ということです。

　企業は、一人でも多くの人から「ありがとう」をもらうために存在しています。自動車メーカーなら自動車という、便利かつ快適に移動できる道具をつくってくれたことに対して、人々は「ありがとう」と感謝します。パソコン、スマートフォン、靴、洋服、レストランの食事、その他のサービスもそうです。企業は一人でも大勢のお客様からの「ありがとう」を集めるために、さまざまな努力をして製品やサービスをつくりだしているのです。

　では、地域金融機関が人々から「ありがとう」を集めるためには、何をすればよいのでしょうか。

　前述したように、いくら預金を集めたとしても、この超低金利で利息は雀の涙ですから、預金者が喜ぶとは思えません。

　一方、融資についてはたしかに低い金利でお金を借りられるものの、特に地方になるとお金をどんどん借りたいという企業が少ないので、預金と同様に「ありがとう」をたくさん集めるのは困難です。

Of course, regional financial institutions are a private business, and must generate revenues in some way to be sustainable. At the same time, they must readdress the purpose of their business.

To put it very very simply, a company's purpose of existence is to receive as many "thank you's" from as many people as possible. An automobile manufacturer receives "thank you's" from people grateful for the convenience and comfort that the vehicle can provide. Same for computers, smartphones, shoes, clothes, restaurant meals and other services as well. The more "thank you's" that the companies generate from their customers, the more sales and profits they generate.

For regional financial institutions, no matter how much deposits are collected, with the current ultra-low interest rate, gratitude is quite limited.

Loans can be borrowed at low interest rates, but with lower growth prospects, there are fewer and fewer companies that needs to borrow more money. Not too many "thank you's" here as well.

In addition, how many of the people who have purchased mutual funds or insurance products are sincerely happy?

In order for regional financial institutions to gather a lot of "thank you's" from the local community, it appears the shift of mindset from "regional financial institutions" to "regional development institutions" holds the key. In essence, a "pro-

さらにいえば投資信託や保険商品も、それらを購入・加入した人のうち、どれほどの人が心から喜んでいるでしょうか。

　このご時世では、預金も、融資も、投資信託や保険商品も、お客様が喜ぶとは限らない。「そうしたら何も残らないじゃないか」と諦めるのはまだ早い、と私は考えています。

　地域金融機関が地元の人々からたくさんの「ありがとう」を集めるためには、前述したように地域金融機関から地域振興機関という意識展開にヒントがあります。銀行は「前に出すぎてもいけない」。あくまでも黒子に徹し、地元経済が活性化するためのインフラストラクチャーになるのが、これからの地域金融機関の一つの姿だと思います。

　経済的な規模の競争で地域が都市圏と背を比べても意味ありません。しかし、地域には歴史があります。文化もあり、自然も豊富です。人々の暮らしのウェルビーイングに大事な要素がたくさん存在しているのです。

　地域振興機関とは、つまり地域のウェルビーイングの総合プロデューサーのほかありません。

　そして、総合プロデューサーという意味ではすべて自前主義ということではなく、自分たちが得意ではないところは他と組んであたっていく目利きが大事です。統合性は、たった一人で実現できることではなく、まさにSDGsゴール17が示すように、パートナーシップが大事なカギになります。

　その地域の総合プロデューサーである、地域振興機関として手掛けるべき重要テーマは2つあります。1つは「環境」、もう1つは「事業承継」です。この2つの大きな課題解決に向けて、地域金融機関は総合プロデューサーとしてかかわりがもてるはずなのです。

ducer" of revitalization of local economies.

It makes no sense for regional communities to compare themselves with large metropolitan areas like Tokyo. The economic scale is too different. However, regional communities are rich in history, culture and nature. The regional communities have the resources for a lifestyle of well-being.

A regional development institution's role is a "producer" of lifestyle of well-being in the local communities.

The producer does not do all the work by himself, but rather the important skill set is collaborating with others. The integrated approach is all about partnership. Just like Goal 17 in the SDGs says.

As a producer of regional development, one important theme is the "environment" and the other is "business succession".

環境問題解決のプロデューサーとして

　以前、大分県の津久見市に講演で訪れました。ここは人口2万人足らずで、大分県のなかでは最も人口が少ない市です。

　この土地では石灰がとれるのですが、それを運ぶためのベルトコンベアが町中を通っていて、街を囲む山を削って採掘された石灰石がそれに乗せられて港の近くまで運ばれていきます。港の近くには石灰石を加工する工場があり、そこで加工された石灰が船に乗せられ、出荷されていきます。そのような工場が5、6カ所ほどあるので当然のことながら、特に街の規模や人口に対してCO_2をたくさん排出しています。

　もちろん、それに対して地元企業は何も対策をしていないというわけではありません。地球温暖化に影響を及ぼす二酸化炭素を発生源で捕集して封じ込める「カーボン・キャプチャー」の試験的な取組みを始めていると現地の経営者から聞きました。

　とはいえ、カーボンニュートラルの街づくりというところまで思考が飛躍していないように感じました。時代の大きな流れはすでに決定されている状況です。その流れに取り残されないよう、民間の地域振興機関の立場から誘導し支える役割はあるのではないでしょうか。

　渋沢栄一はいいました。「**すべて世の中の事は、もうこれで満足だという時は、すなわち衰える時である**」（『渋沢栄一 訓言集』国家と社会）

　地元から「われわれは、ずっとこうやってきた。これからも高望みすることなく、ずっとやっていければよいのだよ」という声が聞

Producer for Solving Environmental Issues

Tsukumi in Oita Prefecture is a city of less than 20,000 people, where the primary industry is limestone. Limestone is excavated from mountains surrounding the city and pass through the town on huge belt conveyor encasements to the port to be shipped away. There about 5 or 6 factories, and even though Tsukumi is a small city, their factories must be emitting large volume of CO_2 into the environment.

Of course, this does not mean that local companies have not taken any measures. A local factory manager told me that they are running pilot project for "carbon recapture."

However, the vision for carbon-neutral still quite limited, even though the tides of changes are quite apparent in the world. There must be a role that a regional development institution can play here.

Eiichi Shibusawa said, **"When all are satisfied, it is time for decline."**

If voices such as "We've been doing this for a long time, and we don't need to stretch," can be heard from the local community, then the role for the producer of the regional development is very clear. First, presenting the risks of being satisfied with the status quo and the opportunities for clean environmental development.

The Japanese government has committed to a carbon-neu-

こえてきたら、地域の総合プロデューサーの役割は明らかだと思います。まず、満足というリスクについて、しっかりと理解していただくことに努めなければなりません。

日本政府は2050年までにカーボンニュートラル、つまり脱炭素社会の実現を目指すことを宣言しました。それを実現するためには掛け声だけでは駄目で、現状の満足に陥っても駄目です。二酸化炭素を排出する産業の技術革新などの努力が必要です。

自動車製造業界では自社製品である自動車および部品の製造の工程から排出される二酸化炭素をできるだけ減らすべく、ガソリンで動く内燃機関の自動車から、電気とモーターで動く電気自動車に主軸を移す「トランジション」が必要になります。銀行にとっては、その移行を支える資金を提供する「トランジション・ファイナンス」という新たな事業チャンスも訪れます。

ただ、それらの産業および企業のトランジションを促進させていくためには、国や自治体、さらには教育・研究機関も巻き込んだ、まさに産官学連携によるプロジェクトが必要になっていきます。こうしたプロジェクトを総合プロデュースする役割を、地域金融機関が担えるはずです。

銀行が担っている金融ビジネスは、いうなれば経済の血流そのものです。経済活動を担っている主体である個人、大企業、中堅中小企業、また、研究機関、自治体、など、その地元におけるあらゆる経済主体と何かしらの取引をもっているのが、銀行をはじめとする金融機関です。

専門性の深さという点では決して深いとはいえないかもしれません。ただ「組織対組織だけではなく、キーパーソンのつながり」、「あの組織だったら、あの人」というアナログ的な経験値を銀行は

tral society by 2050. In order to achieve this goal, just chanting slogans run short and making effort towards technological innovation is of utmost necessity.

The automobile industry will experience huge paradigm shifts from internal combustion engines to electric motors, and the industry needs to "transition." This will require large amounts of investments, hence new business opportunities for "transition finance."

However, in order to promote the transition of industries and companies, it is necessary to implement projects that involve the national government, local governments, and education and research institutions, in collaboration with industry, government, and academia. Regional financial institutions should be in a perfect position to play that role as a producer of regional development.

Finance is the blood flow of the economy. Banks and other financial institutions are in a position to have transactional relationships with all players in the regional economy, such as individuals, large corporations, small and medium-sized enterprises, and sole proprietors, as well as research institutions, local governments.

Bank may not have the depth of expertise in a given sector, but they have a wide experience of the who's who. Not just organization to organization relationships, but the key person at a particular organization. This type of analogue network and experience is invaluable.

もっているはずです。この人間関係に根差したネットワークは、どの経済主体よりも広いものをもっています。

　このネットワークつながりの観点で、私は2008年からオープン型で主宰している「論語と算盤」経営塾を地域金融機関向けのプログラムとしても提供しています（http://shibusawa-co.jp/school）。講義だけではなく参加者同士のディスカッションに重みを置いていますので、渋沢栄一の思想の現代意義を学び合う同志として行員と顧客のネットワークつながりの増強にもお役に立っているようです。

　このように、そのネットワークを活用し、ある社会的課題が持ち上がったとき、自分がもっているネットワークのどことどこをつなげば、その解決に向けてプロジェクトを組めるのかといった提案を、地域金融機関は進められるはずです。

　あるいは第1章で述べた北海道の上士幌町のように、再生可能エネルギーの自給率が1,090％もあって、そのうち100％がバイオマス発電というように、再生可能エネルギーが余っているような地域もあります。

　日本国内を幅広くみれば、その土地によって再生可能エネルギーを含むエネルギー事情は大きく違うので、たとえば上士幌町のようにエネルギー自給率の高い自治体から、エネルギー自給率の低い自治体がカーボン・クレジットを購入して、環境対応を進めていくことも、構想の段階でも検討し始めるべきではないでしょうか。

　カーボン・クレジットの取引をグローバルに行うだけでなく、日本という国内でも積極的に取引するようにすれば、カーボンニュートラルの実現可能性は一段と高まるでしょう。このように、異なる自治体間でのカーボン・クレジットの取引を行うところで、地域金融機関がプロデュース役として積極的に介在していけば、地域振興

I have been offering RONGO and SOROBAN study sessions since 2008, and have tailored it to regional financial institutions as well. (http://shibusawa-co.jp/school) It is not lecture-style, but rather group discussions, which is helpful in fortifying the network.

Regional financial institutions can and should leverage their vast network to offer solutions and projects whenever social issue is raised.

In the case of Kamishihoro-cho in Hokkaido that I mentioned in Chapter 1, their renewable energy supply to local demand ratio is a whopping 1090% and there are other areas in Japan where renewable energy generation is surplus as well. It seems logical that market of trading carbon credits from region to region should be developed.

As regional development institutions, in collaboration with local authorities and regulators, banks can and should take the lead role as the producers for making this new market.

機関としての存在感を高められるはずです。

事業承継問題解決のプロデューサーとして

　もう一つ、地域経済が直面している大きな問題があります。それが事業承継です。

　日本企業の99.7％は中小企業といわれており、文字どおり日本経済の屋台骨を支えているのですが、その多くの企業で経営者が高齢化する一方、後継者難に陥っていて、廃業を余儀なくされるケースが増えてきています。

　2017年に経済産業省が発表したデータによると、日本に存在している約380万社の中小企業のうち、「もうすぐ社長が引退を迎えるが、後継者が決まっていない会社」を廃業予備群として抽出したところ、全体の3分の1に当たる約127万社がそれに該当したという話があります。

　もし、この約127万社がこのまま本当に廃業ということになったら、日本経済に及ぼす影響は甚大なものになります。たとえばこの127万社分の従業員が、仕事を失うことになります。経済産業省のデータによると、650万人の雇用と22兆円のGDPが消失されると考えられています。

　少し前の話になりますが、岡野工業株式会社が2018年に廃業しました。この会社は蚊が血を吸うための口と同じ太さの3ミクロンの注射針を開発し、「痛くない注射針」として有名になった会社です。従業員3人の小さな町工場ですが、年商は8億円で、たくさんの特許ももっていました。そういう素晴らしい会社でしたが、後継者が

Problem Solving for Business Succession

A critical problem facing the regional economies is that of business succession. It is said that 99.7% of Japanese companies are SME's (small and medium-sized enterprises). Hence, they are the backbone of the Japanese economy.

According to data released by the Ministry of Economy, Trade and Industry (METI) in 2017, of the approximately 3.8 million SME's in Japan, about one third or 1.27 million reported that the owner will soon retire but no successor has been identified. The potential loss of employment at these companies is estimated to be as high as 6.5 million people, or 22 trillion yen of GDP.

In 2018, a company called Okano Kogyo Co., Ltd. closed its business. This company developed and manufactured "non-painful injection needle" of 3 microns in diameter, the same size as that of mosquitoes. It was a tiny factory with just 3 employees, but the annual business was 800 million yen, and lots of patents. But there was no successor, and they shut their doors.

Small businesses like this will probably increase towards 2025. At that time, 2.45 million owner-management of SME's will be over 70 years old.

おらず、結局は廃業せざるをえませんでした。

こういう事例が、これから2025年にかけて増えてくるおそれがあります。2025年になると、70歳以上の経営者が245万人にもなるからです。この人たちは、後継者が見つからなければ廃業を選ぶおそれがあります。現在、日本が大きな時代の節目に立っていることは明らかです。

後継者不在に陥っている中小企業であっても、そこの技術ノウハウなどの価値が市場経済で評価されているものであれば、その会社の経営権を譲渡するという手があります。つまりM&Aです。

M&Aというと大企業同士の大型の買収案件が報道を賑わせますが、実は中堅どころの中小企業同士のM&Aも活発に行われています。

ただ、中堅どころの中小企業を対象にしたM&Aであっても、買収金額が数千億円といった巨額資金が動く案件ではないため、外資系のM&Aバンカーや日本のメガバンク、大手証券会社は扱いません。だからこそ、中小企業のM&Aをメインに扱う「M&Aブティック」が、このマーケットで大きなシェアを握っているのですが、そうだとしたら地域金融機関でも十分、このマーケットでできることがたくさんあるはずです。

M&Aが資本や財務的なロジックだけで成功する可能性は低いと思います。会社には生の人間が存在していて、大企業と比べて中小企業における「人間」の存在感はさらに高い。だからこそ、ウェットな「あの組織だったら、あの人」という目利きが大切な付加価値となるのです。

これから中小企業の後継者問題がさらに深刻化していくのは明らかですから、この分野で地域金融機関が果たせる役割は非常に大き

Even though SME's cannot find successors to the business, if their technology, manufacturing and other skills can be valued in the market economy, there is a chance of continuity through M&A (Merger and Acquisitions).

M&A among SME's has become quite active, but because their size, it does not attract interest from big M&A banks. It is usually boutique brokers handle such deals. This certainly looks like an area that regional financial institutions could play a more active role.

M & A is unlikely to succeed if it is only based on financial logic. There are real people in a company, and the presence of "human resources" is likely to have even higher impact for SME's compared the larger companies. That is why the "for that organization, this is the person" type of knowledge by the regional financial institutions becomes very important.

Boutique M&A brokers do not have the financial functions and are merely intermediaries. However, regional financial institutions do have a financial function, in addition to the people knowledge. It is clear that this is a field that a regional development institution simply cannot overlook.

くなります。M&Aブティックの場合、金融機能はもっていませんから、あくまでも仲介業務にとどまりますが、地域金融機関には先ほどの「あの組織だったら、あの人」に加え金融機能があるので、買収企業のファイナンスも含めてさまざまな関与の仕方があるはずです。M&Aは、地域振興機関の役割が期待され、ますます重要になることでしょう。

自らの統合も重要な課題 ～～～～～～～～

　統合性という観点から地域金融機関の役割を考えたとき、これから深く関与していく社会課題として環境問題と事業承継が考えられます。これは前述したとおりですが、地域金融機関がわが身を振り返ったとき、自らの統合についても真剣に考えなければなりません。地域金融機関の経営統合は、金融業界にとってこれから大きな課題になっていくでしょう。

　すでに現在進行形ですが、地方から大都市圏への人口移動は、これからも続くでしょう。それに伴って、地域によっては人口がますます減少し、経済活動はさらに低迷していくおそれがあります。地域経済が低迷すれば、銀行からお金を借りる人、企業は減る一方になりますから、地域金融機関の存在意義もなくなっていきます。

　現在のように、各都道府県に地方銀行と第二地方銀行、信用金庫、信用組合というように、さまざまなレイヤーの金融機関が存在する必要性は、後退していく傾向になっています。

　そうなったとき、地域金融機関の経営統合が現実味を帯びてきます。すでに複数の地域金融機関が経営統合を進めていますが、今

Integration of Regional Financial Institutions

As discussed above, environmental issues and business succession are very important social issues regarding regional communities. Another critical issue is the integration of the regional financial institutions, themselves.

Based on the size and industry of the borrowers, various layers of financial serves offered by first tier regional banks, second tier regional banks, shinkin banks, and credit unions, still exist in each prefecture. Yet the need for such layering of lenders is receding.

Therefore, the business integration of regional financial institutions is becoming a reality that cannot be avoided. Some are already pursuing business integration, and this trend will accelerate further in the future.

However, in many cases, the holding company structure is created and multiple regional financial institutions just hanging below, and the benefits of integration are not so clear.

後、この動きはさらに加速していくでしょう。

ただ、すでに行われている地域金融機関の経営統合をみると、統合メリットに課題もあるでしょう。地域金融機関の経営統合というと、持ち株会社をつくり、その下に従来のまま複数の地域金融機関がぶら下がっているだけというケースが多いように思えます。

たしかに経営規模は大きくなるでしょう。でも、それだけで果たして経営統合のメリットが得られるのかというと、その点が疑問です。たとえばバックオフィス部門を本体から切り離して統合するという考えがあってもよいと思います。

バックオフィス部門はどの金融機関でも基本的にすることは同じなので、最も差別化を図りにくい業務です。つまり、この部分を統合して規模を倍増したからといって、他の金融機関と競争するうえで特に優位性が生じません。むしろ2つのシステムがそれぞれのレガシーのまま同時進行するとかえって問題のリスクのほうが高まるでしょう。

渋沢栄一は『論語と算盤』の「勇猛心の養成法」で、このような指摘をしています。

「要するに我が国今日の状態は、姑息なる考をもって、従来の事業を謹直に継承して足れりとすべき時代ではない」と。

銀行員のみならず、人々は今日の一日の過ごし方は昨日の過ごし方と同じであって、明日の過ごし方は今日の過ごし方と同じであることに甘んじ、基本的に変化を好みません。しかし、時代は必ず変化し続けます。したがって、自分たちの生活や仕事の過ごし方を持続させるには、時代の変化に対応しなければならないということです。

そうだとしたら、まず複数の地域金融機関がもっているバックオ

In theory, there should be scale-merit from integration. However, the question is whether the benefits of business integration can be achieved by increasing size alone. A more rigorous management restructuring plan of separating out business units and integrating the back-office operations should be considered more.

Fundamentally, the back-office operation should be the same for any bank and doubling the size of these functions alone cannot reap benefits of integration. Complexity will rise if two systems continue to operate with their own legacy, supposedly under the same roof.

Eiichi Shibusawa said in his speech titled "Cultivating the Brave Heart" that "**In short, the state of our nation today is not such that we should be satisfied just to faithfully accept the ways of the business from the past.**"

It is not only the bankers, but everyone would rather spend a today that was the same as yesterday, and a tomorrow that is the same as today. People basically do not like to change old habits.

However, time always keeps on changing. Therefore, we must actively adapt to the ever-changing world, in order to sustain the ways of our lives and work.

To adapt to the demands of the changing times, integrating back-office operations into one seems like the logical option to pursue. There should be significant cost reductions, and the management can focus their valuable resources in sectors

フィス部門を統合して、そのうえで、それをまるごと外部に業務委託してしまえば、間接部門のコストが大幅に削減できるはずです。そして、余裕ができたキャッシュフローによって、それぞれの地域の特徴にあわせられる、自らの特長を活かせる部門に経営資源を特化すべきではないでしょうか。

さらにいえば、地域金融機関の経営統合は地理的に近いところにある金融機関同士で統合するケースが多いと思うのですが、この点もあまりこだわる必要はないはずです。

昔のように、インターネット・テクノロジーが発展していない時代であれば、地理的条件は経営統合をするうえで重要な意味合いをもっていたかもしれません。ただ、いまはインターネットによって地球の裏側でも即時にコミュニケーションがとれる時代です。

それを考えれば、たとえば北海道と沖縄県の地域金融機関同士で経営統合をするという選択肢も生まれてきますし、そのほうがお互いの地域的な縄張りを意識することなくシナジー効果をあげやすい可能性があります。

個々の地域金融機関の「勝負どころ」はDX（デジタル・トランスフォーメーション）を目的化することではありません。規模を優位性にもつデジタル・プラットフォーマーに地域金融機関が勝てるわけがないからです。

むしろ、DXは手段として活用しながらも地域金融機関の目利きである、長年、地域で築いてきたアナログ・インフォメーションを活用した総合プロデューサー事業を目的として勝負すべきです。

where the bank's unique characteristics can be tailored to the characteristics of their regional communities.

Furthermore, regional financial institutions tend to favor integration with others that are geographically in nearby regions. This may have had important implications for business integration in the past when communication tools were limited, but these days the choices of internet-based tools are vast. One can communicate freely with someone on the other side of the planet, so why not throughout Japan?

For instance, there should not be any physical barriers for the integration of financial institutions in Hokkaido and Okinawa Prefecture. By being separate geographically, the merged banks won't be fighting over the same turf in a nearby territories, and hence find more ways increase synergies.

For regional financial institutions, DX (Digital Transformation) should not be an objective for competition since there is little chance against the huge digital platforms that already have scale advantages. Rather, DX should be used as a means to achieve the objective of conducting business as a producer of regional communities.

人材育成が急務 〜〜〜〜〜〜〜〜〜〜〜〜〜

　問題は、地域金融機関のなかに、この手のプロデューサー役をこなせる人材がどのくらいいるのかということです。

　実はこの点が、やや心許ないというのが現実です。なぜなら、これは地域金融機関に限ったことではないのですが、組織の規模がある程度大きくなると、業務の効率化を図るために、部門がどんどん細分化されていくため、専門分野の知識に秀でている人物は大勢いても、部門を横断的に見ることのできる人材がいなくなってしまうのです。

　これはある地域金融機関の経営トップがおっしゃっていたのですが、これからの銀行員のするべきこと、あるべき姿として、5つのポイントがあげられるということです。

　第一が、人と人をつなぐ場をつくること。まさに総合プロデューサーの仕事そのものです。

　第二が、ちょっとおもしろかったのですが、「寄ってたかって」。つまり、同質ではない大勢の人でチームを組み、一つのことにあたるということ。

　第三が、おせっかいを焼く。これも総合プロデューサーの仕事です。いろいろなところに首を突っ込み、人と人をつなげていく。紹介していく。

　第四は、先駆者の真似。そのためには人に会う必要があります。会って教えを乞う。学ぶ。そこから新しいアイデアが浮かんできます。

　そして第五に、アウェイ感のあるところで自分を磨くこと。地元

Urgent Need for Human Resource Development

The role that regional financial institutions must play is that of a producer of regional development. The question is, however, how many bankers working in regional financial institutions are capable of this role.

This is an area of concern, not just limited to regional financial institutions, but for any organization that grows in size, and the wall becomes higher and higher. This wall makes it more and more difficult to see and reach across internal resource to deliver the best service to the regional community.

Top management of a regional financial institution shared his views of what bankers should strive for. He listed five.

First, create a place to connect people. This is exactly the work of a producer of regional development.

Second, swarm. In other words, a team of diverse members swarming towards the same goal.

Third, be nosy. Poking around in various places and connecting people to people.

Fourth, imitate the pioneer. Find that right person, ask for their guidance, and learn. From there, new ideas will emerge.

Five, go somewhere "away." Being burnished by new experiences is important. Nothing new will be born, just by

の居心地のよいところで動いているだけでは何も新しいことは生まれません。

　いずれにしても、皆が支店のなかだけで大半の時間を過ごし、預金と貸出の残高を伸ばすことだけを目標にして、達成して終わりということだけを繰り返しているのでは、総合プロデューサー役をこなせる人材を育成することはできません。営業目標という数字を達成した人を高く評価するのはいままでの金融機関ですが、これからの新しい時代を切り拓く人材を育成するためには、この評価軸も変えていく必要がありそうです。

　人材を育てるにあたっては、ちょっと荒療治かもしれませんが、前述した後継者難に陥っている中堅中小企業に30代前後の若手の行員を出向させ、できるだけ経営に近いところで働かせるという手も考えられます。そこで経営者としてのセンスを磨いてもらうのです。ポイントは、銀行色に染まった年齢になってから別の産業の経営の舵取りをすることでなく、別の産業色を銀行に取り込むことです。

　もし本人がそこで社長になりたいとなったら、社長として活躍してもらえばよいでしょうし、一定期間、経営する側で修行をした後、金融機関に戻ってきてもらって、経営幹部候補として働いてもらうのもよいでしょう。こうした人材育成法を取り入れれば、後継者難の問題の解決にもつながりますし、同時に銀行にとっても人材育成につながります。

　「統合性」には、いうまでもなく経営トップのコミットメントが重要なカギを握っています。

　たとえば地域金融機関が経営統合をするにあたって、バックオフィスを統合するという話になったとき、経営トップが「システム

staying put in cozy places.

Spending most of the time inside the branch office and repeating daily routines is not a way to develop human resources for a producer of regional development. In order to cultivate human resources that can braze open a new future, it is necessary to update evaluation methodology.

Sending promising young bankers in their 30s to SMEs that are in need for successor can be one method of human resource development. Working close with the owner management and experiencing his struggles will be an important investment for the career of the young banker, and as such for the bank.

The key is not sending seasoned bankers who can only talk and act like a banker to the SMEs. It is much more important to bring back the sensibilities and color of the SMEs back to the bank.

If the young banker eventually becomes the successor of the business, that is good for him as well as the bank. If he comes returns to the bank, with his added experience on the outside, he should be placed on track for higher management positions at the bank.

Needless to say, commitment of top management holds the key to any integration. For instance, if top management leaves the decision to the experts in systems, then back-office system integration will never occur. People are people. There will be a tendency favor protecting their work and po-

についてはよくわからないので、すべて現場に任せる」ということ
になったら、恐らくバックオフィスの統合は永遠に実現しないで
しょう。

　なぜなら現場は自分たちの仕事を守ろうとしますから、それが統
合され、なおかつ外に出されるとなったら、絶対にそれを進めよう
とはしません。

　「か」の力を極めながらも、最終的に組織の不確実性の要素が多
い、見えない未来への飛躍と現実をつなげる「と」の力は、統合性
に不可欠な経営者の決断力、そのものです。

sition, rather carrying thorough with integration.

While skillfully utilizing the power of "OR," ultimately connecting the uncertain future to reality is the power of "AND." This is essential for decision making in the integrated approach.

透 明 性
―インパクトのメジャーメント―

Chapter 5 ● Transparency
— Measurement of Impact —

透明性とは情報開示のこと？

　普遍性、包摂性、参画性、統合性というように話を進めてきましたが、これらをすべて機能させるためには、その土台として、しっかりした「透明性」を確保する必要があります。

　逆にいうと、透明性がしっかり確保されていなければ、他の４つの要素は成り立たないことになります。

　渋沢栄一は『論語と算盤』の「合理的な経営」で自身の透明性の考えを示しています。

「現在有るものを無いといい、無いものを有るというがごとき、純然たる嘘を吐くのは断じてよろしくない、ゆえに正直正銘の商売には、機密というようなことは、まず無いものと見てよろしかろう」

「会社の内部は一つの伏せる魔の殿と化し去り公私の区別もなく秘密的行動が盛んに行われる。真に事業界にために痛嘆すべき現象ではあるまいか」

　お話をお伺いした地域金融機関の経営トップも断言されました。「やっていることをちゃんという。隠匿しないだけではなく」

　では、透明性とは何なのでしょうか。なぜ透明性を確保しなければならないのでしょう。この疑問の由来するところは、「信用できないからすべてを開示しろ」ということだと思います。

　投資家が企業に対して、財務諸表をはじめとする経営関連の数字の開示を求める理由は、「ひょっとしたら企業は、自分たちにとって不利なことを隠しているのではないか」という不信感があるからです。

Does Transparency Mean Disclosure?

In the last four chapters, we have talked about universality, inclusiveness, participatory approach, and integrated approach, but in order for all these things to work properly, we need to ensure "transparency and accountability."

Eiichi Shibusawa expresses his own ideas regarding transparency in "Rational Management" of *"Rongo and Soroban."*

"To say you have when you have not, and to say you do not have when you do, are certainly not proper. Therefore, in order to conduct honest and proper business, it is fair to say that there is no such thing as secrecy."

"If the inside of the company has turned into a temple of a lying demons, and secret actions are actively performed without distinction between public and private, that is a very regrettable condition for the business world."

A president of a regional financial institutions I interviewed also affirmed the same. "Let's say in truthfulness, what we are doing. Not concealment."

The reason why investors seek disclosure of financial statements and other management-related figures is to mitigate the risks of being misled.

However, one point of difficulty with disclosure is that

しかし、ここが非常にむずかしいところなのですが、情報を開示したからといって、開示した相手がちゃんと真意を汲み取ってくれるかという問題があります。

　たとえば、企業が自らの財務情報をすべて開示したとします。売上げ、流動資産、固定資産、経常利益、税引き利益、純利益、流動負債、固定負債など、さまざまな勘定科目があり、それぞれに金額が記載されていますが、それを見て企業の経営の実態を精度高く把握できるアナリストや投資家はもちろん存在していますが、地域金融機関の他の多数の大切なステークホルダーで実際にどの程度いるでしょうか。

　つまり企業側が「私たちはこうして財務諸表の中身を完全に開示しており、透明性を維持していますよ」といくらいっても、それを見る人たちが中身の意味を何も理解できていなかったら、この情報開示は透明性確保につながっていないことになります。

　また、企業の価値はすべて財務的な価値で表せているかというとまったくそうではありません。

　企業の価値＝財務的な価値であれば、すべての上場企業の PBR（株価純資産倍率）は1.0のはずです。B とは Book、Value は純資産のことであり、すなわち純資産（企業の資産から負債を引いた財務的な価値）であり、株式市場の価値評価が財務的な価値にとどまるのであれば、株価が示す時価総額と純資産は同額になるからです。

　しかし、実際のところ、株式市場は企業のいままでの事業活動が可視化されている財務的な「見える価値」だけではなく、これからの成長性も株価に織り込みます。

　したがって、成長性を見込んでいる企業に対して、株式市場の評価は成長プレミアムを加え、PBR は1.0以上の倍率になります。企

even if the information is disclosed properly, that does not mean the reader will understand the true intentions.

For example, let's assume that the company discloses its financial information in great detail. There are some analysts and investors who can accurately grasp the condition of the company, based on the information provided. However, how about the other important stakeholders for the regional financial institutions. Do they really understand or care what all the numbers mean?

In other words, even when the company discloses their financial information with the intent of great transparency, if the stakeholders in the community do not understand the meaning of the contents, is this disclosure ensuring transparency? Probably, not.

It is also important to add that value of a company cannot be fully expressed only in terms of its disclosed financial value.

If corporate value where to equal its disclosed financial value, then the PBR (Price to Book Ratio) of all listed companies should be at 1.0.

B stands for Book Value of the company, i.e., net assets (financial value of a company's assets minus liabilities). If the stock market values the company from financial value only, then the market capitalization (stock price) and net assets (financial balance sheet) should be the same amount.

However, in reality, the stock market not only reflects the

業の財務的な価値に加え、非財務的な「見えない価値」への期待の表れともいえます。

　ただ、この考え方は、上場している銀行に対して深刻な課題を株式市場から突き付けられています。なぜなら、ほとんどの銀行のPBRは1.0割れです。PBRが0.5割れの上場地方銀行も、多数あります。

　現在の財務的な価値と比べると将来の価値が減っていることを見込んでいるという株式市場から警告です。つまり、将来性がなく、これからの企業価値が毀損するという評価です。

　そして、企業の非財務的な「見えない価値」を一言で表すと、それはその会社の未来をつくっている経営者や社員、つまり人材です。

　そう考えると、きわめて厳しい観点になりますが、株式市場の判断は、上場しているほとんどの銀行で働いている人材は、企業価値においてネガティブ効果しかないと示されていることになります。

　この株式市場の価値判断にはすべての銀行が反論するはずです。

　「いやいや、わが銀行には、優秀な人材がたくさんいる。市場の、株主の価値判断が間違っている」と。

　私も銀行には大勢、優秀な人材が誠実に懸命に働いていらっしゃることに間違いないと思います。そのような方々を大勢、個人的に知っていますから。

　しかし、その価値が見えない株主や市場が悪い、という意見には賛同できません。銀行が自分たちの最大の財産である「人」の価値を市場で可視化できていないことが、現実にあると思います。

　株式を上場しておらず、会員が出資者である信用金庫や信用組合が、「それは上場している地銀さんの問題」と他人事のように突き

financial "visible value" of the companies that can be seen through results of their business activities, but the stock market tends to price in growth potential in the future into current stock prices.

Therefore, for companies with growth potential, stock market valuations will add on a growth premium and PBR will be higher than 1.0, its theoretical financial value. It can be said that this future growth premium is in fact the non-financial "invisible value" of the company.

However, this approach poses serious challenges to banks that are listed in public stock markets since most banks trades less than PBR 1.0. There are many that are as low as PBR below 0.5.

This means the stock market is expecting banks to destroy corporate value to below its current financial value in the future.

And if one were to describe the essence of the company's non-financial "invisible value" in one word, it is human resources. Without the directors and employees, the company cannot create value into the future.

This is a very severe message that the stock market is sending to the regional financial institutions. In effect they are saying that human resources at banks only have negative impact on corporate value.

Of course, all banks will strongly refute this judgement by the stock market value. "We have many many talented peo-

放すことも賛同できません。

　いろいろな意味で透明性が制度化によって確保されている上場会社である地銀がそのような状態であれば、信用金庫や信用組合の会員などステークホルダーへ自分たちの価値がきちんと可視化できているとはいえないからです。

　実際に「株式会社でないことは弱点である」と認める経営トップもいらっしゃいます。とある信用金庫の理事長は会員8万人に経営状況を理解していただくために、年に2回、74店の支店長とともに総代会員の代表の説明に回っていらっしゃるようです。

　実践上、透明性とは単に情報を開示するだけではありません。

「ちゃんと説明する」

「ディスクロージャー（情報開示）だけでは顧客の反応が見えない」

「レポートを発行するだけでなく、何をやっているかの内容を発信する機会をつくることが大事」

　このような声が、お話をお伺いした地域金融機関の経営トップから相次ぎました。

　では、透明性を高めるために、どうするか。

　まず価値の可視化には「フレーミング」が必要です。やや象徴的な話になりますが、瀬戸内の直島に「無限門」という李禹煥氏の近代アート作品が野外展示されています。平べったい巨大な金属のアーチが緑に囲まれた小谷に展示され、その内側から瀬戸内海が展望できます。人によってはただの人工物のアーチにしか見えず、意味がわからないでしょう。

　しかしその作品の存在がそこになければ、その場所から眺める瀬戸内の景観を同じように楽しめなかったかもしれません。景色は

ple working here. The market, the shareholders are wrong."

I agree that there are many excellent people working at regional financial institutions with determination and integrity. I know many of them personally.

However, I cannot agree with the opinion that shareholders and markets are "wrong." I think the reality is that banks have not been successful in making sure that the markets can see that their "people" are in fact their greatest asset.

And if shinkin banks and credit unions, who are not listed entities believe this is not their problem, then I cannot agree with that opinion either.

Because regional banks are listed public companies there are certain requirements for transparency. If they are having problem with showing their true value, the inclination is to believe that shinkin banks and credit unions are having the same kind of problems vis-à-vis their stakeholders as well.

In fact, some top management at these firms admit that "not being a public company can be a weakness" in terms of transparency and governance.

In order to make sure that their members fully grasp their business conditions, the top management of a shinkin bank goes around 2 times a year to have face to face meetings to explain their business conditions to the representative members of their 74 branches.

Therefore, in practice, transparency is not simply about disclosing information.

まったく変わっていない、しかし「無限門」のフレーミングによっ て、見えていなかった美しさが可視化できたのです。

このフレーミングという概念に、数値化がむずかしい企業の非財 務的な、見えない価値の可視化のヒントがあるようにも思います。 見えない価値の正しい「答え」を定めることは困難ですが、わから ないことに啓発されて「問い」を繰り返すことが、とても大事だか らです。

しかしフレーミングは、「無限門」のように、その特定の場でし か体感できないというサイト・スペシフィックの課題があります。 そこで必要になってくるのが、「トランスレーション」という概念 です。

デジタル技術の発展により、情報のトランスミッション（伝達） の効率性は著しく向上しています。成果を測定する数値化は、まさ に情報のデジタル化であり、数字は万人の共通言語となります。

ただ、正確にいうと、数字は共通言語に「なる」と断言できな く、「なるはず」としかいえません。なぜなら、情報の送り手が体 感しているコンテクストが受け手にも体感できないようであれば、 同じ数字を見ても意味が通じないからです。

だから、銀行と顧客、本部と支店が同じ情報の意思伝達ができて いない場合があるのかもしれません。

情報を伝達するだけではなく、意味も含めて「翻訳」するトラン スレーションが必要であり、その正確性はアナログ的な感性に宿り ます。

どういう意味か。少なくとも、透明性とは数字をただ見せればよ いということではない、ということです。

その数字の意味をトランスレーションする、人の関与がより重要

"Explanations need to be thorough."

"Just by disclosing information, we cannot see reactions from our customer."

"It is important not only to publish reports, but also to create opportunities to communicate."

These voices echoed one after another from the top management of regional financial institutions.

So, how can transparency be improved?

First of all, "framing" is necessary in order to see the value. This is a somewhat a symbolic explanation, but there is an open-air exhibition of Lee Ufan's piece of modern art called "Mugen-mon" (Infinite Gate) on Naoshima Island in Setouchi. It is a huge flat metal arch that is on display in a small enclave facing the sea and surrounded by greenery.

The beautiful Setouchi Inland Sea can be enjoyed when you view the arch from landside. Some may only see it as an arch, just an artificial object. Many may wonder why this is considered "art."

However, if the piece work was not displayed in that enclave, I might not have been able to enjoy the scenery of Setouchi Sea from that place in the same way. The scenery has not changed at all, but the framing by the "Gate" has allowed me to see and experience the beauty that I will not have otherwise seen.

I think that this concept of "framing" offers hints for seeing non-financial "invisible values" of companies. You need

になります。トランスレーションとはコミュニケーションの力や意識向上、そのものです。

　日本の会社は自分たちのことを「ウチ」と表現することが多いです。ウチでは価値が暗黙の了解でわかっていたとしても、それはまさにサイト・スペシフィックであり、ウチ以外には意味がわかりません。

　地域金融機関のウチで見ている価値を、ソトにも意味が通じるようにトランスレーションする。この工夫や意識の向上がきわめて大事だと思います。

　SDGsの5つの原則を通じて、地域金融機関の存在意義であるパーパスを表現することが本書のねらいでありますが、そういう観点では、この「透明性」という概念を自分コトとするのが最も重要かもしれません。

　情報を開示しただけでは、マジックミラーのようにウチから見せているつもりでも、ソトからは透明性はありません。単に情報を開示するだけでなく、相手が意味も理解できるトランスレーションの工夫によって初めて、透明性が確保できるのです。

a "frame" of reference to see the value.

Trying to arrive at the correct "answers" for "invisible values" may be difficult, but like much of modern art, "questions" arise when confronted with point of reference or a "frame." Stimulating the question is an important aspect of transparency, not just the answers.

However, with "framing" there is a problem of being "site specific." You are able to see the beauty of Setouchi because you are there, for instance, in front of the "Infinite Gate." This is where the concept of "translation" is needed.

With the development of digital technology, the transmission of information has significantly improved. Quantifying measurement of results is precisely the digitization of information, and the number is a common language for all.

However, if the context of the experience of that information is lost, then the digitized information that was transmitted to another might not make sense for the recipient.

For instance, the bank and customers, headquarters and branches may be looking at the same numbers, but if the context is lost in translation, then either side may not be on the same page.

It is therefore necessary not only to share the information, but also to "translate" it, including meaning, texture and contents, all in the realm of analogue sensibility.

Transparency is not about just showing the numbers.

In order to translate accurately the meaning of that num-

統合報告書にみる透明性のかたち

　企業が自社の透明性を確保する方法の一つの工夫として、「統合報告書」があります。

　株式を上場している企業は皆、「有価証券報告書」を定期的に作成し、誰でも閲覧できる状態にしておく必要があります。試しに、

ber requires the human touch. Translation is the power of communication and awareness.

Japanese companies often describe themselves as "uchi" (inside, like a house). If you belong to the "uchi", you understand often without explicitly expressing it in words. However, this skill set is very very site-specific. If you don't belong to the "uchi," you don't understand.

Therefore, value that one understands within the "uchi" of the regional financial institutions needs to be translated to communicate with "soto" (the outside).

The awareness of the need to improve this kind of translation skills are extremely important.

Just disclosing the information, is like a one-way magic mirror. From the inside, you thought you were being transparent, but from the outside, you were not. Transparency can only be ensured, not only by disclosing the information, but also by devising ways of translation so that others can understand true meaning.

Transparency by Integrated Reporting

One way in which companies are innovating their transparency is through integrated reporting.

All listed companies are required to publish their annual "securities reports" and disclose it to the public. On any

どこかの上場企業のサイトに入って、「IR 情報」のタブをクリックしてみてください。ちなみに「IR」は Investor Relations、つまり投資家の窓口担当です。

その企業の IR サイトに入った後、必ず「有価証券報告書」という項目がありますので、それをクリックします。そうすれば直近の IR 資料を閲覧できます。

見ればわかると思いますが、なかなか読み進めるのが困難でしょう。それは、有価証券報告書の記載内容、記述方法などがすべて決められていて、ドライな読み物だからです。

そこから大きくはみ出した記載内容、記述方式をとることは認められていません。試しに複数の上場企業の有価証券報告書を比べてみるとよいでしょう。会社は違っても、形式はほとんど同じです。

なぜ、このような形式になっているかというとアナリストや投資家など株式市場の参加者にとって企業情報が「横比べ」できたほうが効率的で便利だからです。つまり、有価証券報告書は上場企業の対話のために用意しているものとはいえません。

これに対して統合報告書は、発行が義務づけられているものではありません。書式も自由です。したがって、企業は自分たちの好きなように、自分たちの仕事に対する想い、熱意などを盛り込むことができます。

つまり有価証券報告書でいう、大半が数字で語られているものをトランスレーションして、誰もが最後まで飽きることなく読み進められる仕立てに各自企業が工夫するのが、統合報告書なのです。

したがって、統合報告書は「つくって満足」ではいけません。大事なのがブラッシュアップです。

website of a listed company, click the tab for "IR" (investor relations) in order to access "securities reports". It may be a difficult read for many of those who are not trained in the investment profession.

The contents of the securities report from different companies look all the same, with the same formatting. Basically, boring for the casual reader.

The formatting leaves little flexibility of expression because the function of this report is comparability with other companies. It is more efficient for analysts and investors to compare the information horizontally to other companies. In other words, securities reports are not prepared with intent of dialogue with the reader. It's basically the numbers, and the narrative is purposely dry and limited.

In contrast, the integrated report is not a requirement for listed companies. Because the format and content of the report is up to the companies, they can be more creative in their forms of expression.

In other words, the integrated report is where the company can experiment with their "translation," so that the reader can read through the report, without getting bored, and come away with an understating of true corporate value.

Integrated reports are important communication tools for a wide range of stakeholders, including shareholders, customers, business partners, and employees of the company. It is also important to recognize that publishing the report is

統合報告書は株主や顧客、取引先、あるいは自社の従業員も含めてさまざまなステークホルダーを想定読者とした大事なコミュニケーションツールです。したがって、一度発行して終わりではなく、常に想定読者が何を感じたのかを把握して、「刺さった」内容、関心をもたれなかった内容をしっかり精査し、次に発行する時、そのフィードバックを活かす必要があります。

　といっても、1年前と今年で企業が伝えたいメッセージがそんなに大きく変わらないのも事実です。統合報告書に掲載しているストーリーが毎年大きく変わるようでは、むしろそのほうが心配です。なぜなら、それだけ会社が大きくぶれていることの証左みたいなものだからです。

　したがって、統合報告書の内容は、1年タームでみた場合、「何が変わったの？」と思われるくらいの微細な改善修正でもよいかもしれません。

　でも、対話からのフィードバックを反映した改善をしっかり行うのと行わないのとでは、5年後、10年後の内容に大きな違いが生じてきます。改善に常に取り組む積極的な企業の統合報告書は、5年後、10年後という少し長い期間を置いてから両者を比較したとき、この企業が何に力を入れてきたのかというストーリーが明確に読み取れるようになるのです。

　地域金融機関で株式を上場している地方銀行などは、いま一度、統合報告書の制作にチャレンジしてみればいかがでしょうか。任意のステークホルダーとの対話ツールという意味では上場会社に限定される必要なく、信用金庫や信用組合が制作してもまったく問題なく、むしろ取り組むべきでしょう。

　また、「ブランドブック」のように銀行としていま何を考え、ど

not the end, but a part of a continuing process to improve content.

The story of the corporation will not change dramatically year to year, but it gives opportunity for the reader to observe the longer term trend, say 5 to 10 years, of the company to see whether there are any changes in narrative with changing business environment.

Regional financial institutions should think about trying their hand in producing integrated reports.

There are also some regional financial institutions that will put together their "Brand Book" which is a good way to convey their core corporate principles in very plain language.

Expressing more creativity on their corporate website is another form of improving communication skills. All institutions have their webpage on the internet, yet most of them are not something that you might want come back to over and over again.

Maybe there are some fixed self-biases that financial institutions should not be fun and creative in expression, especially in serious matters such as transparency. This is frankly a shame.

If the purpose of a regional financial institution is revitalizing their regional communities, why not show that vision with expression. Why not share that vision with others in the community and the world to see.

ういう経営哲学、経営方針をもっているのか、といったことを非常に平易な言葉で伝える小冊子をまとめて製本している地域金融機関もあります。

それ以外にも、たとえば自社のサイトの工夫でもよいでしょう。どの地域金融機関も自分のところのホームページをもっていると思いますが、「また見に行きたい」と思わせる内容が多いとはいえません。

金融機関だから、そんなにおもしろおかしいものをつくることはできないという固定概念が、透明性を抑制しているかもしれません。たとえばコミュニティを活性化させる活動に地域金融機関がかかわったことで、「これだけの笑顔が生まれたのですよ」ということを表現する映像なり、テキストなりを用いたコンテンツがあってもよいと思うのです。

実際、地元で商売をしている人たちからすれば、地域金融機関から事業資金を融資してもらっている人もいるでしょうから、自分の商売を通じて地域金融機関とのかかわりを実感できると思うのですが、たとえば学生や専業主婦、あるいは一般企業に勤務している人の大半は、地元にある地域金融機関が地元経済にどのような貢献をしているのかなど、ほとんどわからないと思います。

それだけに、地域社会、強いては世界中の誰もが見てわかるようなかたちで、自分たちが行っているビジネスの中身を、より多くの人に知ってもらうようなかたちで透明性を打ち出す必要があるのです。

密室の意思決定を避ける

　透明性の問題は行内にもあります。前述で金融機関のウチとソトの課題を指摘しましたが、実は地域金融機関のウチには「暗黙のカースト」が存在している風土が一般的でありましょう。

　これは金融機関というよりも、日本企業のすべてからみられる傾向の一つなのですが、「阿吽の呼吸」で命令が伝達されたり、物事が決定されたりするケースが往々にしてあります。この手の命令伝達や意思決定は、透明性とは真逆の、不透明極まりないものといえるでしょう。

　たとえば頭取を含めた役員会議の場は、実はそこでいくつかの議題について話し合うのではなく、すでに根回しによって決定されていることを発表する場であるという話を聞いたことがあります。

　根回しといっても、事前に「今回の役員会議ではこういうことについて話し合います」という情報共有や事前説明までなら問題ありませんし、むしろそれは会議の参加者が事前準備を行うために必要なことだと思うのですが、会議で決定されるところまで根回しされているのは、やりすぎだと思います。そのようなことが横行していたとしたら、政治家の「密室政治」を誰も批判できません。

　ある地域金融機関は役員会議の透明性を高めるため、事前の根回しを廃止しました。根回しや阿吽の呼吸で物事が決まってしまうと、どうしてもいいたいことをいえない雰囲気ができてしまいます。なので、その地域金融機関の経営トップは、会議の決定は事前の根回しをいっさいせず、あくまでも会議の場で決めることを徹底しました。

No Behind Closed Doors Decisions

There are also in-house issues regarding transparency such as an "implicit caste." This is a general characteristic for all Japanese companies, not just financial institutions, where orders and thoughts are implicitly transmitted rather than through explicit verbal transmission.

Therefore, the decision-making process is often rather opaque. Much of the important decisions are made internally beforehand and the board of directors meeting just rubber stamps the decision.

In order to reform this in-house mode of decision making, one of the presidents of a regional financial institutions decided to implement a no more "nemawashi" rule. In effect, no prior counting-of-the-votes type of discussions regarding important decisions before board meetings.

He wanted to put clear away the atmosphere of not being able to say what you want to say and make sure that it was not stupid to voice opinions contrary to the majority.

Eiichi Shibusawa agreed. He said, "**In today's world, everything is a majority vote, a majority vote, and overwhelming the few is easy. That is cruelty.**"

「担当外が発言できない、マイノリティが発言できない」

「決まっている話や主流に反対しづらい」

このような風土が継続するのは地域社会の繁栄という金融機関のパーパスにそぐわない、という問題意識による方針転換だと思います。

渋沢栄一も、このようにいっています。

「今の世の中では、　何事も多数決、多数決というけれども、多数の力で少数の者を圧倒するは、これほど容易のことはない。またこれほど残酷のことはない」（『渋沢栄一　訓言集』・道徳と功利）

地域経済を活性化するためにインパクトある説明責任が必要

透明性に関する話の最後に、「アカウンタビリティ」について考えてみたいと思います。

アカウンタビリティは「説明責任」などと訳されています。本来、説明責任とは、たとえば企業がある投資を行うにあたり、「この投資にはこのようなリスク、不確実性があり、最悪の場合でこれだけの損失が生じるおそれがある。しかし、一方でこれだけのアップサイドが期待できる」といったことを、株主や取引先、顧客、あるいは従業員も含めて、それらのステークホルダーにきっちりと説明することを意味します。

ところが最近の金融機関をみていると、「説明責任があるから、逆に何もしない。リスクもとらない」というケースが、ある意味では決まり文句になっています。

たとえば、リスクをとる必要がある融資案件があったとして、そ

Impact Accountability for Revitalizing Regional Economies ⟨⟨⟨⟨

Accountability is usually is defined as "responsibility of explanation." In essence, accountability is an explanation about the uncertainty or risk regarding outcome to stakeholders involved. For example, "In the worst case, this much loss will occur, but on the other hand, we can expect this much upside."

However, the sad reality that in many cases, the internal narrative at the financial institution is as follows.

"Because there will be accountability, I do not want to take risk."

"I don't want to execute that loan because it looks like it will require a lot of explanation, and that is troublesome."

Unfortunately, this type of situation is not a rarity.

の融資を実行するかしないかを決めるとき、「いちいちリスクを説明するのは面倒だし、ステークホルダーに説明して納得してもらうのは骨が折れるから、何もしないほうがいい」という判断が下されるケースは例外といえるでしょうか。まさに説明責任という言葉を逆説的に解釈した好例といってもよいでしょう。

日本初の銀行をつくった渋沢栄一は『青淵百話』の「元気振興の急務」で唱えています。

「其の日其の日を無事に過されさへすればそれでよいといふ順行のあるのは、国家社会にとつてももっとも痛嘆すべき現状ではあるまいか」

栄一が現在の「事なかれ」が常識となっている金融機関の意思決定のあり方を見たら、相当の怒りを示すのではないでしょうか。

「事なかれ」が横行したら、地域金融機関の存在意義がなくなります。地域経済を活性化させるのが、地域金融機関の大事なパーパスです。それを実行するためには、地域活性化のためのビジネスに対して、不確実性はあるけれども、資金を融通する役割を積極的に担っていく必要があります。「事なかれ」では駄目なのです。

だからこそ、まっとうな説明責任とは何かということを、特に地域金融機関はしっかりと考えるべきでしょう。そのうえで、この説明責任という言葉をもっと前向きにとらえ、ステークホルダーとの信頼関係を構築して、地域経済に貢献できる組織体をつくっていくことが求められているのです。

現在、ESG（E環境、S社会、Gガバナンス）への意識が経営や資本市場で高まっています。2005年ぐらいから国連の議論から生じた考えでありますが、当時は専門家やスペシャリストの領域であり、特殊な人たちが特殊なことをやっているというイメージしかありま

Eiichi Shibusawa, who established the first bank in Japan, was an advocator of "Urgency of Vitality."

"Is it not a most sad situation for the state of the nation, if it is okay just to let the days pass by without a care?"

No doubt, he would be quite angry if he saw the state of financial institutions, as described above.

"Just letting the days pass without care" is not an option for regional institutions who are committed to their purpose of revitalizing their regional communities.

That is why it is so important for regional financial institutions to understand what "accountability" truly means. Being able to assume "responsibility" should be addressed in a more positive context, something which is an important contribution to the well-being of the regional economy.

At present, awareness regarding ESG (Environment, Society, Governance) is gaining momentum in corporate management and capital markets. ESG was a concept that arose from discussions at the United Nations around 2005, but at that time, it was a field for the experts and specialists. It was seen as an area where special people were doing special things.

Now, with the changing times, ESG has taken up the center stage among corporate management and capital markets.

To many people, however, ESG tends to mean simply the disclosure of non-financial value of a company. However, as

せんでした。しかし、時代の変化により、現在、ESG は経営や資本市場の意識の中心部にきています。

ESG を企業の非財務的な価値の情報開示という観点でとらえる傾向があります。ただ情報開示だけでは不十分であるということを前述しました。実際のところ、世の中では ESG の次の流れがすでに始まっています。

それは、インパクトのメジャーメントです。

第1章で「インパクト投資」のことを簡単にご紹介しました。社会的インパクトを意図し、その継続のために経済的リターンを求める、『論語と算盤』の現代意義です。

そして、社会的インパクトの意図の要になるのが「メジャーメント」（測定）です。どのような社会的インパクトがあるかを、数値化したメトリクス（測定基準）で表現するという考え方です。

たとえば、教育事業に取り組んだため、教育のアクセスが何件増えて、その影響で何名が高度教育を受けることができて、その影響で生涯所得が何ドル上昇したか。単純な例ですが、このような考え方です。

言い換えれば、インパクト・メジャーメントはインパクト投資のアカウンタビリティです。経済的リターンだけでなく、社会的インパクトの成果の可視化です。

ここで重要なポイントは、この「インパクト・メジャーメント」とはインパクト投資という特殊な人たちが特殊なことをやっているという次元でなく、ESG の次の流れとして世の中で始まっているということです。

「ESG 情報を開示しているということだけではなく、インパクトをメジャーメントしていますか」

discussed earlier, information disclosure alone is not enough. As a matter of fact, the next trend of beyond ESG is already beginning in the world.

It is the measure of impact.

We briefly touched upon the concept of "impact investing" in Chapter 1. Impact investing is the modern-day translation of *"Rongo and Soroban."* The intent is social impact, but it seeks economic return for sustainability of the operation. And the essential expression of this intent is "measurement," quantifiable metrics for social impact.

For example, in a very simple case, increase in access to education, and as a result increased number of people in the community attaining higher education, and because of receiving higher education, the impact on lifetime earnings.

Impact measurement is the accountability of an impact investment. With measurement, you can see the social value of outcome as well as that of economic returns.

It is important to note that trends in "impact measurement" indicate that it is not just for special people doing some special things, but rather on a track to be the next thing, beyond ESG.

"Are companies measuring impact, not just disclosing ESG information?"

"If the companies are measuring impact, are they goal setting for impact?"

This is exactly the concept of accountability.

「メジャーメントしているのであれば目標設定として定めていますか」

つまり、まさにアカウンタビリティの概念です。

実は現在、世の中では、従来の会計制度に環境インパクトおよび社会的インパクトを反映するという先駆的な試みが始まっています。現状では、まだ試験的な考えであり、環境インパクトや社会的インパクトを貨幣化して、財務的な価値とともに企業会計制度に反映させることに多くの課題があります。

業種も異なる、規模も異なる、地域も異なる特異性がある多様な企業を、同じ環境インパクト・社会的インパクトのメジャーメントで表すことは非現実的であるという反論もあるでしょう。

ただ、興味深いことがあります。現在の当たり前と思われている企業会計の起源は社会における過去の大きなショックです。1933年のアメリカの大恐慌です。当時、企業の透明性、アカウンタビリティを高めなければならないとの社会的要請が起こりました。

そして、多くの企業から反論がありました。業種も異なる、規模も異なる、地域も異なる特異性がある多様な企業を一つの測定基準で表すことは非現実的である、と。

でも、多様な企業の財務的な価値を一つの会計制度のメトリクスで表すことはいまでは当たり前になっています。そして、現在、新たな大ショックが世界で走っています。新型コロナウイルスの感染拡大による世界規模ショックです。

ということは、数十年後に振り返ったときに、環境インパクトと社会的インパクトが企業会計制度で計上されていることは当たり前になっているかもしれない、それはあの時にコロナ禍という大ショックが世界であったから、という意見もあります。私も、その

In fact, there are already pioneering research to reflect environmental and social impacts into traditional corporate accounting. At present, it is still an experimental idea, and there are many challenges to reflect environmental and social impacts into the corporate accounting alongside financial value.

Some will likely argue that it is impractical to represent a variety of companies in different industries, different sizes, and different geography with the same measurement of environmental and social impact.

This is true. But it is interesting to note the origins of corporate accounting as we know them today met the same kind of arguments at the start. It was the great shock of the Great Depression of America in 1933. At that time, there were demands from society that companies should be more transparent and accountable.

And there was the same kind of rebuttal from the companies. It is impractical to use a single metric to represent a variety of companies with different industries, different sizes, and different geographies.

Well, that is the standard now in financial corporate accounting. And now there is another big shock today. The Covid-19 pandemic.

Looking back from couple of decades from today, there is possibility that of measuring environmental and social impact of corporations for accounting of corporate results start-

可能性はあると思います。

　この企業の環境的・社会的アカウンタビリティをインパクトとして会計制度に反映する研究に世界的にリードしているのは、米ハーバード大学ビジネス・スクールの Impact Weight Account Initiative（IWAI）というプロジェクトです。

　この IWAI プロジェクトに日本企業として共同研究の第一号として手をあげたのは、企業ガバナンスや非財務的な「見えない価値」の可視化に長年積極的に取り組んでいる製薬会社のエーザイ株式会社です。これから IWAI ジャパンの設立の視野も入っており、他の先駆的な日本企業の参加を募ります。

　「知らないところで、また新しいルールが決まっている」とぼやくだけではなく、そのルール・メイクのプロセスに日本企業が参加することに、これからの時代のために大切な意義があると思います。

　IWAI ジャパンの参加に地域金融機関も手をあげるべきではないでしょうか。「豊かな地域社会の発展」というきわめてインパクトある事業のアカウンタビリティを世界基準で反映することに大義ありです。

　現に、ふくおかフィナンシャルグループは SDGs 支援子会社「サステナブルスケール」を2021年の３月に設立しています。ここの「スケール」とは「尺度」の意味合いがあるようです。まさにアカウンタビリティを表すインパクト・メジャーメントと類似している考え方です。

　私は、たった３つの言葉を地域金融機関のみならず、日本社会の産学官すべての組織から NG 語として排除したら、新規事業の発

ed because of that big global pandemic shock of 2020-21.

Impact Weight Account Initiative (IWAI) at Harvard Business School is the recognized global leader in the study of the impact of environmental and social impact in accounting systems. EISAI Co., Ltd., a pharmaceutical company that has been a frontrunner in corporate governance and reporting non-financial "invisible values" in corporate Japan was the first Japanese company to raise their hands to participate in a joint research project with IWAI. There is also a movement starting to establish IWAI Japan, that will encourage other pioneering Japanese companies to participate in this new field of accounting practice.

It is critically important for the new era for Japanese companies to participate in the rule-making process, not only to complain that "new rules gets decided some place we did not know about."

If IWAI Japan is established, I would encourage regional financial institutions to join. The purpose of regional financial institution of "developing the well-being of regional communities." This is critically an impactful business and if accountability measures can stand up to global standards, that would certainly be a worthy cause.

In fact, Fukuoka Financial Group established Sustainable Scale, a subsidiary supporting SDGs activities, in March 2021. "Scale" refers to measurement of sustainability, a very similar concept to impact measurement and accountability.

足、かつ、透明性やアカウンタビリティも高まり、SDGsが達成されるべき2030年には「イケている」会社組織がたくさん増えていると信じています。たった３つの言葉です。

「前例がない」

「それは組織に通らない」

「誰が責任とるんだ」

この３つの言葉が、日本の地域金融機関および会社組織が豊富に抱えている優秀な人材の可能性を抑制しています。あまりにももったいないです。

誰一人取り残さない世の中という飛躍を実現させるSDGsのバッジを付けるのであれば、まず、この３つの言葉を口から発することをぜひともやめましょう。

I believe that if 3 phrases are eliminated from the Japanese vocabulary, not only from regional financial institutions, but from all organizations of industry, academia and government in the Japanese society by 2030, there will be lots of "cool" Japanese companies, launching new businesses, with transparency and accountability. Just only 3 phrases!

"There is no precedent."

"That will never will never get approval through the organization."

"Who's going to take the responsibility?"

These 3 words have been limiting the potential of talented people in Japan's regional financial institutions and corporate organizations for way too long. Much too wasteful.

If you want to put on the SDGs badge that is pledging to "leave no one behind" from our world, let's start by not uttering these 3 phrases.

あとがき―すべて常識です―

SDGs バッジを付け続けましょう

　最後までお付き合いいただき誠にありがとうございました。ここまで私の乱文にご一緒していただけたということは、SDGs という壮大な人類の目標が、地域金融機関が取り組んでいる「豊かな地域社会の発展」につながっているということに共感を覚えていただいたということだと思います。

　ローカルの常識とグローバルの常識に異なりがあることは確かです。しかし、渋沢栄一は『論語と算盤』の「常識とはいかなるものか」で、このような指摘をしています。

　「智、情、意の三者が各々権衡を保ち、平等に発達してものが完全の常識であろうと考える」

　洋画の名作である「オズの魔法使い」ではカンザスという田舎で平凡な常識な日々を過ごしていたドロシーちゃんが竜巻に巻き込まれ、「オズ」というひっくり返ったような非常識な国に放り込まれます。ドロシーちゃんはカンザスの家に帰るため、自分が失った常識を取り戻すために、冒険を繰り返します。

　そこに三者が現れます。脳がほしいカカシ、ハートがほしいブリキの木こり、そして、勇気がほしいライオンです。つまり、「オズの魔法使い」という映画は、主人公が失った常識を取り戻すには三者の助っ人、智・情・意が必要であることを示してくれます。

　つまり、時代を超える、東西を超える、ローカルでもグローバルでも通じる人類共通の常識が存在しているということです。

Afterword — It's All Common Sense —

Keep On Wearing that SDGs Badge !

Thank you very much for staying with me till the end. This probably means that you agree with my notion that the mutual goal for all humankind around the globe, the SDGs, and the goal of the regional financial institutions to enrich the development of their regional communities, are in fact aligned.

It is true that the norms of the local community and the norms of the global community differ. However, Eiichi Shibusawa says the following "**Common sense is the development of the knowledge, the emotion and the will, all in balance.**"

In the classic movie, "The Wizard of Oz," Dorothy, who was living a normal everyday life in rural Kansas, is suddenly swept up by a tornado which lands her in Oz, a wacky world that makes absolutely no sense to her.

She wants to go home, back to Kansas, to regain the common sense that she has lost.

Help arrives. The scarecrow, who wants a brain. The tin man, who wants a heart. The lion, who wants courage.

The essence of the narrative of "Wizard of Oz," is that when one loses her/his common sense, she/she needs three

さて、ここで智・情・意を三角形の角として表現した場合、中国思想の**中庸**について考えてみましょう。智・情・意を三角形において、「中庸」のポジションとはどこをイメージしますか。

　真ん中というイメージが真っ先に浮かび上がった方が多いでしょう。

　ただ、私の友人で中国古典の専門家である守屋淳さんから「中庸」という概念は「足して二で割った」、つまり、「真ん中」のところではないと教えていただいています。

　「中庸」とは多くの関係性のなかで「ベスト」なポジションを示す場所のようです。

　つまり、真ん中がベスト・ポジションとはいえません。特に同じ二次元の真ん中に中庸を置いてしまうと、智・情・意のお互いの関係性が把握しづらいかもしれません。

　むしろ、「中庸」とは同じ二次元のポジションではなく、三次元のピラミッドの頂点ではないでしょうか。ここに「中庸」を置けば、智・情・意の関係性が一目瞭然なベストなポジションになります。

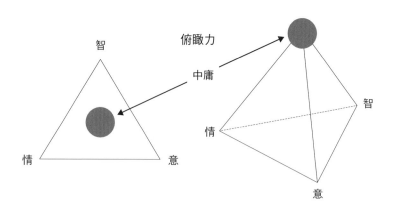

helpers, knowledge, emotion and will.

This is the common sense of humankind that can transcend the times, East and West, as well as local and global.

Now let's position knowledge, emotion, and will as three corners of a triangle. Where would you place the **golden mean** (Zhongyong), which is a well-known doctrine of Confucianism.

May be right in the middle? After all, it is the "mean."

Well, according to Atsushi Moriya, an expert in ancient Chinese philosophy and a good friend, the "golden mean" is not like "adding and dividing by two." It is not the middle ground. It is more like "the best position" in various circumstances. After all, it is "golden."

The middle ground is not necessary the best position. If you position yourself in the middle of a triangle, it might be rather difficult to see the relationship among the corners because you are in the same two-dimensional space.

However, if you put yourself at the peak of a three-dimensional pyramid, then the relationship among the three corners of the triangle is easily recognized. Clearly, this apex position is the best, therefore that is where the "golden mean" should be positioned.

I was thinking about this revelation of the "golden mean," when I was chatting on-line with Kumi Fujisawa, Director of SophiaBank, Ltd, a think-tank. Kumi was helping me to organize my thoughts for this book in autumn of 2020. She

この「中庸」に関する思考回路が、本書の内容をまとめる際に去年の秋に真っ先にオンライン取材でご協力いただいた、シンクタンク・ソフィアバンク代表の藤沢久美さんの一言とシンクロしました。

　地域金融機関を含む複数の上場企業の社外取締役を務め、20年以上、多くの経営者と接点をもつ藤沢さんがおっしゃるに、「日本の経営者は与えられた任務を真面目に執行し、事業内容の隅々もきちんと把握されて本当に立派である」と。ただ、いつも足らないところがあると感じるという指摘でした。

　藤沢さんいわく、それは**俯瞰力**。経営者自身が任されている領域と異なる、世の中の情勢、時代の流れ、文化などの角度から自分の仕事を見渡す視点です。

　つまり、「俯瞰力」とは、異なる次元からベスト・ポジションの視点をもつ「中庸」とまったく同じ概念ではないでしょうか。

　そういう意味で、**"論語"** が社会の軸で、**"算盤"** が経済の軸として表現したときに **"論語と算盤"** のポジションを二次元で描いてしまうと、「真ん中」といういちばんおもしろくない場所に置いてしまいます。したがって、**"論語と算盤"** も「中庸」のように異なる三次元の頂点から見渡すベスト・ポジションでありましょう。

　また **SDGs** の達成も、ローカルかグローバルの軸、できるかできないかの軸という二次元で判断するのではなく、SDGs が達成できているムーンショットの状態も、「中庸」のように異なる三次元に置かれたベスト・ポジションといえるでしょう。

　そして、同じようなベスト・ポジションから、地域金融機関で日々の業務に務めている二次元の自身が見渡せている頂点からの視点が**パーパス**。

is an independent director of several listed companies in Japan and has a wealth of experience of over twenty years with corporate executives.

She basically has high regards for corporate executives in Japan. They are very diligent with their assigned posts and have good understanding of business areas that they are responsible for. However, she told me that there is a shortcoming that she often encounters.

That is the lack of the **bird's-eye view.** The perspective of seeing their business from a different dimension, such as world affairs, transition of norms, culture, etc.

I realized that this "bird's-eye view" is exactly the same position as the "golden mean."

This means that if one were to draw the RONGO the society axis and the SOROBAN the business axis in two dimensions and you place **RONGO and SOROBAN** in the middle, that is probably the most uninteresting position. The best position is probably the same as the "golden mean" position, the apex in a three-dimensional figure.

And, if you draw achievement of **SDGs** by "local-global" axis and "can-cannot" axis in two dimensions, the best position here is also the moonshot position in three dimensions, the same as the "golden mean" apex position.

Finally, where is the **purpose** of regional financial institution in relationship to daily tasks at hand? Well, that is also the apex best position of the "golden mean."

地域金融機関の**パーパス**、**SDGs**、**"論語と算盤"**、俯瞰力と**中庸**のすべてが類似的な概念であるような気がしてしようがないですが、皆さんはいかがでしょう。このまとめにご賛同いただけるのであれば、ぜひとも SDGs バッジを付け続けてください！

　さて、藤沢久美さんから始まり、去年2020年の秋には多くの地域金融機関の多忙な経営トップから貴重なお時間をいただき、オンライン取材にご協力をいただきました。おかげさまで、本書の内容に私では見えなかった重要な視点が与えられました。心より御礼を申し上げます。

〈取材日付順、肩書当時〉

　　めぶきフィナンシャルグループ取締役　小野訓啓さん

　　京都信用金庫理事長　榊田隆之さん

　　九州フィナンシャルグループ代表取締役社長　笠原慶久さん

　　静岡銀行代表取締役会長　中西勝則さん

　　北海道銀行代表取締役頭取　笹原晶博さん

　　ふくおかフィナンシャルグループ執行役員　五島久さん

　　第一勧業信用組合理事長　野村勉さん

　　西武信用金庫理事長　高橋一朗さん

　また、金融行政の視点から、金融庁前長官の遠藤俊英さんから大変示唆に富むお話を賜ることができたことを大変感謝しております。

　そして、最後になりますが、本書の取材・構成にご協力をくださった鈴木雅光さん、企画立案を頂戴したのに原稿をお返しするのに長らくお待たせしてしまった株式会社きんざいの山本敦子さん、執筆を支えてくださり本書が無事に完成できたのはお二人のご尽力のおかげです。どうもありがとうございました。

It is very clear to see that the **purpose** of regional financial institutions, **SDGs, RONGO and SOROBAN, Bird's-eye view** and the **golden mean** are all exactly at the same apex position. It's all common sense. If you agree with this observation, keep on wearing that SDGs badge!

After the initial guidance from Kumi Fujisawa in the autumn of 2020, I started a series of on-line interviews with top management of regional banks. The individuals listed below were very gracious to spare their precious time with me. With their help, I gained many perspectives that otherwise, I would not have had. Thank you very much from the bottom of my heart.

(listed in order of interviews, titles as of autumn 2020)

Kunihiro Ono, Director, Mebuki Financial Group

Takayuki Sakakida, President, The Kyoto Shinkin Bank

Yoshihisa Kasahara, President, Kyushu Financial Group

Katsunori Nakanishi, Chairman & CEO, The Shizuoka Bank

Masahiro Sasahara, President, The Hokkaido Bank

Hisashi Goto, Operating Officer, Fukuoka Financial Group

Tsutomu Nomura, President, Daiichi Kangyo Credit Union

Ichiro Takahashi, President, Seibu Shinkin Bank

I also want to express my sincere gratitude to Toshihide Endo, former Commissioner Financial Services Agency for

あとがき

his invaluable insights from the perspectives of a top regulator for financial institutions.

Finally, I want to pay respects to Masamitsu Suzuki who helped me with the on-line interviews and composition of the draft, as well as Atsuko Yamamoto of Kinzai who proposed this book project. Sorry for the many delays with the final draft. I could not have been able to complete this project, without the two of you!

【著者略歴】

渋澤　健（しぶさわ　けん）

シブサワ・アンド・カンパニー株式会社代表取締役、コモンズ
投信株式会社取締役会長
複数の外資系金融機関でマーケット業務に携わり、2001年にシ
ブサワ・アンド・カンパニー株式会社を創業し代表取締役に就
任。2007年にコモンズ株式会社（現コモンズ投信株式会社）を
創業、2008年に会長に就任。経済同友会幹事（アフリカ開発
支援戦略PT副委員長ほか）、UNDP（国連開発計画）SDG
Impact運営委員会委員、東京大学総長室アドバイザー、成蹊大
学客員教授等。
著書として、『渋沢栄一100の訓言』（日経ビジネス人文庫、
2010）、『SDGs投資』（朝日新書、2020）、『渋沢栄一の折れない
心をつくる33の教え』（東洋経済新報社、2020）、『超約版　論語
と算盤』（ウェッジ、2021）ほか。

対訳　銀行員のための『論語と算盤』とSDGs

2021年9月22日　第1刷発行

著　者　渋　澤　　健
発行者　加　藤　一　浩

〒160-8520　東京都新宿区南元町19
発　行　所　一般社団法人 金融財政事情研究会
企画・制作・販売　株式会社 き ん ざ い
出 版 部　TEL 03（3355）2251　FAX 03（3357）7416
販売受付　TEL 03（3358）2891　FAX 03（3358）0037
URL https://www.kinzai.jp/

DTP・校正：株式会社友人社／印刷：株式会社日本制作センター

ISBN978-4-322-13987-7